I0213975

Wealthy Me Academy: Peace Education Freedom tells Minh Hiền and Farshid's compelling educational journeys inspired by Baha'i writings, Buddhist writings, the Bible and philosophers' writings. This book also conveys the stories of Minh Hiền and Farshid's students in rural areas of Việt Nam who have participated in their online courses. The book is illustrated with hundreds of colourful photos. It is released in January 2025 to celebrate the *International Day of Education*.

In memory of our mothers

Lê Thị Kim Nga

and

Shirin Dowlat Imani Hossein Abad

Published in 2025 by Minh Hien Pty Limited
ABN 86 086 458 817
www.minh-hien.com

Inquiries should be addressed to
Minh Hien Pty Limited
PO Box 737
Drummoyne NSW 1470
Australia.

This book is released in January 2025 to celebrate the *International Day of Education* under the brand name *Wealthy Me* ® from the Hobart office of Minh Hien Pty Limited in Albion Heights Drive, Kingston, 7050, Tasmania.

In memory of our mothers.

Creators: Hien Minh Thi Tran (writer) and Farshid Anvari (photographer).

Title: *Wealthy Me Academy: Peace Education Freedom*

ISBN: 978-0-6459782-2-3 (Hardback)

A catalogue record for this book is available from the National Library of Australia

Let your vision be world-embracing,

rather than confined to your own self.

Bahá'u'lláh

Minh Hiền and Farshid at the Baha'i temple, Sydney,
Mồng Một Tết Giáp Thìn, the first day of the Year of the Dragon, 10 February 2024.

CONTENTS

Minh Hiền BE(Hons), MEngSc, GCCA, MCom, GDipMgt, MA, MHE, MEd

Foreword

I am privileged to write the foreword for another of Minh Hiền's books. This time she places on record the motivation, background and results of the generous contribution she and her husband Farshid have made to a fascinating educational program which links them to her village in Vietnam.

In 1981 when I taught Minh Hiền English not long after she arrived in Tasmania after the treacherous escape from war-torn Vietnam, I recognised she was talented student and had great potential (and I told her so!). Now, years later I know her to have many other skills but most importantly she has shown herself to be a talented educator and teacher. With her husband Farshid Anvari, she has established Wealthy Me Academy, teaching Vietnamese students from an impoverished rural background online from Australia.

This latest of Minh Hiền's books tells the story of the many things which led to the establishment of Wealthy Me Academy. She explains how important education is to her family and pays respect to her Vietnamese heritage. The story develops around the key words of love, tenacity, home, youth, mind, education and teaching and how these things have influenced her from a very young age. Along with her search for peace, freedom and education which led to her parents' decision that she should escape to Australia to further the education she was denied in Vietnam, she also describes the significance of colours. This she learned from her mother and it has been a strong influence in her life. Minh Hiền tells her own story including her marriage to Farshid and the trials which they have faced including the tragedy of being unable to have children. Their contribution to education is obvious and the praise of their students makes clear the value placed on their unique style of teaching. The fascinating story demonstrates the generosity Minh Hiền and Farshid have shown over many years and is supported by interesting quotations from a variety of sources and a detailed photographic record.

Minh Hiền and Farshid are indefatigable team and have definitely lived up to Bahá'u'lláh's admonition "Let your vision be world-embracing, rather than confined to your own self."

Margaret Eldridge AM
Sandy Bay, Tasmania, November 2024.

Margaret Eldridge and Minh Hiền at Margaret's home in Sandy Bay, Tasmania, October 2024.

About Minh Hiền and Farshid

Hien Minh Thi Tran (Minh Hiền) is an educator, a researcher and the author of *My Mother* (shortlisted for the 2024 *Furphy Literary Award*), *The Vietnamese Australians* series and *My Heritage: Vietnam fatherland motherland.* She is the recipient of multiple national manuscript development programs: the 2023 Queensland Writers Centre (QWC) *Publishable*, the 2022 QWC *Publishable* (long-listed), the 2021 *Fellowship and Access Manuscript Development* initiative through the QWC, the 2019 *Hardcopy* initiative through the ACT Writers Centre, the 2006 Australian Society of Authors (ASA) Mentorship. She has worked as an engineer, an IT consultant, a systems accountant, a systems manager and a family business manager and owner. While working, she studied for university qualifications in the fields of Engineering, Accounting, Commerce, Management, Arts, and Education and completed a qualification as a professional member of the Australian Society of Certified Practising Accountants (CPA). She holds a Master of Education, a Master of Higher Education, a Master of Arts in Creative Writing, a Master of Commerce, a Master of Engineering Science, a Graduate Diploma in Management, a Graduate Conversion Course qualification in Accounting and a Bachelor of Engineering with Honours from Australian universities in NSW, VIC, QLD and TAS. She is featured in the 2008 *Who's Who in Tasmania*. She has presented academic papers at international conferences and published research papers in international journals in the fields of education, engineering, computing, accounting and management since 1988.

Minh Hiền and Farshid, Sydney, 2023.

Dr Farshid Anvari is a researcher, an engineer and an educational consultant. He visits Việt Nam regularly to learn Vietnamese culture, participate in teaching activities and present papers at international conferences. He holds a Doctor of Philosophy and a Master of Philosophy in Computing, a Graduate Diploma of Information Technology, a Graduate Diploma of Science and a Bachelor of Engineering. He loves to capture the beauty and happiness of life as it is seen through photography.

Wealthy Me Logo

The circle is a symbol of vitality, wholeness, completion, and perfection. The circle represents 'energy while in motion': trust your inner wisdom and use your spiritual gifts.

The colour gold represents strength and wealth.

Lửa thử vàng, gian nan thử sức.

Fire is to test gold, adversity to test human strength.

Vietnamese Proverb

The colour purple represents wisdom, bravery and spirituality. It has been associated with royalty and wealth for centuries. It is 'màu mực tím', the colour of the ink which young Vietnamese students of my generation used for writing their lessons.

The colour light blue represents the *Sky of Hope*. The colour dark blue is for the *Ocean of Generosity*.

The colour orange is for the sun, the sun of honesty. Rising of the sun is associated with renewal and growth. The colour orange represents joy, warmth, happiness, growth, thoughtfulness and having consideration for others.

The colour green is for the bamboo which is associated with nature, renewal and tenacity.

The turtle symbolises longevity, strength and intelligence. The Vietnamese also relate the turtle with their independence. Legend has it that Lê Lợi, who led the Vietnamese to fight against the Chinese invaders in the 15th century, borrowed a sacred sword from the dragon king. After he defeated the Chinese, he returned the sacred sword to the king via the turtle which lived in a jade water lake, the Hoàn Kiếm Lake (Returned Sword Lake) - situated in the middle of Hà Nội.

'Water is fluid, soft and yielding but water will wear away rock,

which is rigid and cannot yield ... what is soft is strong.'

Lao-tzu (around the 4th century BC)

Water is the driving force in nature.

Leonardo da Vinci (1452–1519)

Wealth

O Son of Being!

Thou art My lamp and My light is in thee.

Get thou from it thy radiance and seek none other than Me.

For I have created thee rich and have bountifully shed My favour upon thee.

Bahá'u'lláh, Hidden Words

He is richest who is content with the least, for content is the wealth of nature.

Socrates, Greek philosopher, 470–399 BC

The greatest wealth is to live content with little.

Plato, Greek philosopher, 423–348 BC

It is great wealth to a soul to live frugally with a contented mind.

Lucretius, Roman poet. 94-55 BC

Contentment is the only real wealth.

Alfred Nobel, Swedish engineer, 1833–1896

Wealth is the ability to fully experience life.

Henry David Thoreau, American naturalist, 1817–1862

All riches have their origin in mind.

Wealth is in ideas not money.

Robert Collier, American author, 1885–1950

The Old English word wela, via the Middle English welth, meaning *happiness and prosperity in abundance,* is the root of the noun wealth.

We can only achieve *Happiness and Prosperity in abundance* when we have peace, education and freedom.

We are fortunate to have been able to live in Australia for more than four decades. Australia has given us peace, education and freedom. Through education we have achieved our happiness and prosperity.

Reading and writing are gifts that lead to enlightenment.
Sydney, 2020.

Experiences

Wisdom is the daughter of experience.

Leonardo da Vinci

Italian polymath of the High Renaissance, 1452–1519

The greatest thing in life is experience.

Even mistakes have value.

Henry Ford, Founder of the Ford Motor Company, 1863–1947

Thuyền Nhân Việt Nam (Wooden Refugee Boats) 1979 crowded with men, women and children in heavy seas, watercolour painting on paper by Minh Hiền's niece Ellyse Tran in 2023.

Minh Hiền
Singapore Refugee Camp, 1981.

Seventeen I was,
Learning I was not allowed to acquire,
Cambodia and China my fatherland fought,
Be strong daughter, leave, you must live!
Peace brings happiness,
Freedom brings fairness,
Education brings progress,
Peace, freedom, education bring life,
Be strong daughter, leave, you must live,
Fairness, Knowledge, Virtue you must earn,
Language, to learn and to express,
Be strong daughter, leave, you must live!

In 1980, I sat for the engineering degree entrance examinations at *Trường Đại Học Bách Khoa*, the University of Technology in Saigon.

After the first exam I cycled home and was overwhelmed by a delicious aroma at the doorway. My mother's dressmaking table was covered with colourful food. The dark greens of a mixture of herbs were surrounded by the light greens of coriander and lime at one end. Banana blooms in purple and gold sat in the middle with bright but dark red little chillies competing for attention. At the other end were bright yellow noodles, the vibrant orange of prawns and the brown and gold of sesame rice crackers. These were the ingredients for my favourite food: Quảng noodle soup.

Mama told me to sit at the table. She filled a bowl with herbs and noodles, spread over some prawns and spring onions, and then she poured broth from the steaming pot over the noodles with a serving spoon.

She put the bowl in front of me beside a plate of sesame rice crackers and lemons.

'You need to have the energy to sit for the afternoon exam,' Mama said.

The day the results were announced, I cycled to the university alone.

There was a small crowd at the front gate. I secured my bicycle and joined them.

I searched for my name in the long list on the papers posted on the wall. I recognised a few names from my school. My heart was pounding as I looked up and down the list of names, reading every row.

'Why can't I find my name?' I asked a girl standing next to me.

She told me that I could make an enquiry at the central office and explained how to get there.

I cycled more than ten kilometres to that place, only to be told by the woman at the central office that I was not allowed to study engineering.

'You have two choices, studying for an accounting degree or a diploma in teaching,' the woman said.

'Why?' I asked.

'You are good at maths.'

'I do not want to become a maths teacher.'

'We think you should become a maths teacher or an accountant.'

'Accountant,' I frowned.

She repeated the only two choices available and gave me a form.

'Think about it,' she said. 'If you want to take the offer, answer all the questions in here.'

I took the form.

I never knew why the education board allowed me to sit for the engineering degree entrance exams and then decided that I should learn to teach maths or manage money. I had never considered studying accounting. I did not even know that there was a degree in it. I might have become a very good mathematics teacher, but my father was a teacher and I saw that the respect for teachers had declined as years had gone by. In retrospect, those were two good choices but at the time I was determined to study to become an engineer.

I cycled around the city. It was midday. Saigon was hot. I was drenched in sweat. If it was possible, I would probably have studied law. In my time, the three most valued professions were medicine, law and engineering. My father did not want me to become a doctor. He thought it would be a hard life seeing sick people all the time. And the University of Law had been closed since April 1975.

In reality, at that time, I did not even know what an engineer or an accountant did. I had chosen to study engineering because I excelled in mathematics and I was good at physics and chemistry. No one in my family had been an engineer but I wanted to become one. Decades later I realised the potential of accounting and education and I completed three Master's degrees in these fields.

At home, after I calmed down, I carefully read the form the woman had given me. I saw there were questions about my grandfather, my father and my elder brothers, what they did for their living, where they lived and whether anyone in our family was a member of the Communist Party. Reading the questions listed I realised I would never be allowed to get a higher education degree as three generations of my family were non-partisan.

My father said, 'For years, you have consistently topped your class, so if you cannot get admission into university then I will send you abroad to study. Without an education you have no future.'

I tore up the form.

I asked many friends of my parents and my father's relatives from the North, 'Why did my friend, who did not do as well as I in the examinations, get admitted to the University of Technology to study engineering, but I did not?' Most of them avoided answering my question. But my father's cousin explained, 'You cannot do anything about it because of your family's history. Your father left the North in 1954 and now your elder brothers have left Việt Nam for Australia. You are still young. Wait! In a year or two, things will change.'

My father said, *'Hữu chí cánh thành.'* (Those who have willpower will succeed.) 'I will send you to study in Australia, my daughter,' he added. His tone was positive and he spoke as if he were about to put me on board a five-star grand ship touring the Pacific Ocean.

The night before I left Saigon in April 1981, my father said his sixth sense told him that this trip would be safe. He said that he had also consulted a knowledgeable astrologer who said that my destiny was to live overseas. Papa believed in predictions made by good astrologers and he also studied palmistry. Papa's sixth sense had not failed him in the past.

The long wars had affected everyone. In one way or another, everyone in Việt Nam had suffered, either physically or mentally or both. Some of the effects were visible in physical form. Other forms of suffering were well hidden behind the masks of the hopes and dreams people wore in order to survive. Many Vietnamese believed in life after death, in spirits, ghosts, destinies and palmistry. Papa studied palmistry very seriously. He bought many books on the topic. The accuracy of his predictions often amazed me.

'You should go now,' Papa said. 'Education and knowledge will help you to lead a successful life. I have always had high hopes for you because you are studious and bright. That's why even though you are a girl, I am sending you abroad.'

For some six months, I had felt like a caged bird. Many people I knew had been admitted to university. Some of them used to come to my home at night to learn from me. Now I saw them continuing with their education and here I was stuck at home.

> *Đời cha ăn mặn đời con khát nước.*
>
> The father who eats salty food will have thirsty children.
>
> Vietnamese Proverb

I realised that my future in Việt Nam was doomed. As long as I remained in Việt Nam, my family history would follow me everywhere. Whatever I tried to do, I would have to fill out a form that would ask not only what my parents and grandparents had done, but also where my brothers were and what they were doing.

I had begun to understand why some young people had denounced their families: they had to do it in order to survive. I also realised why some had ended their lives: they had chosen that path rather than betray their families.

Often, when I looked at my mother and saw her bent over the clothes she was making, I thought of how she had done this work day in, day out, for years, long before I was born and was still at it. No, I could not follow in Mama's footsteps.

I would be like a fish out of water, I thought on the last night living in our house in Saigon. The thought of living with my brothers and studying abroad gave me courage. I walked over to the bed and sat down beside Mama. 'I will be fine,' I said. 'I know how to cook. I can cook for the three brothers and I can mend their clothes. I will help my younger brother with his studies.'

'Yes, Mama will feel better,' Papa said, 'living with your brothers, you can remind your elder brothers Tri and Tuệ to study and keep an eye on Bé's studies, too.'

Papa told Mama that he would not be sending Bé off if he had any doubts, and that this was an opportunity I should take. He said that he had engaged trusted friends to check everything from engine to food, petrol and weather. One of Papa's friends was one of the best engineers in Saigon and had been a professor at the best Marine College before April 1975. There would be two experienced men at the helm. Engineers and doctors would also be on board and many knew English.

'You will go with two daughters of Mr Ngọc,' Papa said. 'He has followed the BBC News regularly and he said that US Navy ships are presently touring the Pacific Ocean. Do you know what Mr Ngọc said?' Papa's tone suddenly became enthusiastic. 'He said, "This is a unique opportunity! If you can organise this escape I'll send my daughters. My son can wait!"'

Mama asked me if I had had my period.

I told her that it had only just started that day, and so it would be a bit of a mess to be on a ship, but I would manage it. I had no idea of the conditions I would face.

I imagined I was going to board a big ship, safe and comfortable.

Mama wiped her tears, and her eyes showed huge relief. I did not understand the reason behind her question, too preoccupied with my own thoughts.

'If the worst happens,' Papa said, 'stay calm and seek out a doctor.'

'You must live,' he whispered.

I nodded, though I did not understand what he meant.

I left Việt Nam in a small fishing boat with my fifteen-year-old brother Bé.

Sitting in the small fishing boat, as I remembered Papa's words, I felt a bit calmer and, I hoped that he was right.

I prayed for an American ship to rescue us before any disaster could befall our boat.

I must have dozed off or the fear was so great that my mind went blank.

Suddenly, I heard Bé screaming in a most joyous voice: Hiền, we are safe!

'American ship!' Someone else shouted.

'Hiền, we are safe', I opened my eyes and saw Bé's happy face.

'Come up and see. Let me hold your hand.'

There were tears in my eyes as I heard Bé's excited voice.

Many others also called out in joy.

The sailors threw a makeshift ladder over the side of the giant ship. Some sailors climbed down and assisted us one by one to climb up. Children were carried by their adults and by sailors as they climbed up.

I sat on the deck, looking at the ocean, under the beautiful moonlight, until very late. I felt at peace. But, I also felt homesick. I could not stop thinking of my parents, my sisters, my friends and the people in my hometown. I missed Mama's lovely voice as I recalled my childhood poems. I looked out to the ocean: it was so vast and the waves were so powerful. I felt so tiny. I felt so lonely. While I was deep in thought, a sailor approached me. He must have noticed that I did not join any activities. He tried to get me to smile. He kept on saying "Smile" but I could not understand him. He took out his note pad and a pen to draw a smiling face. Then I smiled. He sketched an ocean, a ship and pigeons then showed them to me. I thought that he was trying to tell me that I should not worry and that I now had peace.

I smiled. I was happy. I did not know his name. I did not know who he was.

He, like other sailors, would meet people like my brother and me only once in their lives. Yet he showed concern. I was touched by his kindness. He gave me a few US dollar notes and a cross. I thanked him in Vietnamese.

We were at sea for two days. When we landed and were about to leave the ship, I looked for him to say goodbye. I could not remember what he looked like because all the sailors looked the same in their uniform. I do not remember his face, but I still remember the crew and all the kind sailors who saved us when we were in the most dreadful situation, at the lowest point in our lives.

Years later I was happy to learn that the whole crew of the USS John Young had received the Humanitarian Service Medal.

I was pleased to read in John Sanness' 1981 Nobel Peace Prize speech to the Office of the United Nations High Commissioner for Refugees (UNHCR) that 'They acted according to the moral law of the sea: you are not allowed to sail past men, women and children in peril on the sea, abandoning them to the perils of wind and wave, to hunger and thirst, to pirates and sharks.'

Minh Hiền and her younger brother were rescued by the U.S.S. John Young in 1981.
Oil painting on canvas by Ellyse Tran in 2021.

It felt eons since our family was parted.

Days turned into years. We were not just separated by the ocean but a giant wall of ideology that had made communications difficult. My father was able to call us from a public telephone at the main Post Office in Saigon on only a few occasions. He spoke in code language while my mother stood beside him in the telephone booth. She did not speak.

Papa said, 'She cries when she hears your voices.'

In April 1986, I stood with my eldest brother Tri and my younger brother Bé at the Hobart Airport.

My heart was racing with happiness as I wondered how I would spend my time in the coming months and what I would do during summer when I finished my studies as I was in my final year of an engineering degree. I would have plenty of time for celebration. Tết would be the first of these occasions.

It is the time of peace, reunion and celebration. I would go out for grocery shopping and cook special meals. I loved the scents of ginger, spring onions, mung beans, coconut, brown sugar, sesame seeds, sticky rice flour and tapioca that used to flow out from Mama's kitchen. I would ask Mama to teach me how to cook the special foods for Tết.

When I was a child, she told me the meanings of the delicious dishes that she made for this occasion. The square shape of the pork pieces and the round shape of the duck eggs in Thịt Heo Kho Trứng (Braised Pork with Eggs) symbolise *vuông tròn đều đặn, mọi sự bình an* (wealth and abundance of a prosperous year ahead). Gỏi Đu Đủ với Tôm Thịt (Pawpaw Salad with Prawn and Pork) is associated with *đầy đủ, thịnh vượng* (fullness and prosperity). Măng Xào Bò (Stir-fried Bamboo Shoots with Beef) is associated with *làng quê kiên cường* (village humbleness and resilience). Above all else, I longed to hear my mother's voice again.

I stood at the tarmac's terminal entrance, looking out through the glass door, watching people, one by one, as they appeared at the doorway of the plane. My eyes scanned each face as they started their descent down the stairs.

My second-eldest brother, Tuệ, appeared at the doorway. Tuệ had flown to Melbourne to make sure my parents would not be lost in transit. My father, dressed in a brown suit, was standing beside Tuệ. I could not see my mother.

When the airport staff lowered the platform, for a moment I did not recognise the person that I saw, familiar face, with snow white hair sitting in a wheelchair. I was shocked to realise that she was my mother. All of her beautiful black hair had turned white. A floral scarf covered her neck but, as it blew aside, I could see she wore a supporting collar.

I was dumbfounded. But I saw that she had preserved her deep characteristics - her dark-blue pants reminded me of the colour of the ocean, the colour of generosity, and her sky-blue jumper, the colour of hope. Mama was smiling. Her beautiful smile never left her.

Tuệ collected my parents' luggage, which was a large aluminium box on wheels, a typical box, in olden times people who travelled by boat carried one. Tri stood quietly, his eyes moving from Mama's wheelchair to the box, then he told Bé to take care of the box.

Tri paused for a moment and walked towards Mama, lifted her out of the wheelchair and carried her in his strong and steady arms. Her head was on his chest. Tuệ pushed the empty wheelchair behind Tri. Bé pulled the aluminium box.

Mama smiled. I could see happiness in her eyes.

Tuệ opened the car's back door and Tri set her down. He put the seatbelt around Mama. She said some words. We looked at each other. We could not understand her.

Papa said, 'Mama says she is very happy. Tri is so strong. No one carried her in Việt Nam.'

Tri, with great difficulty, had managed to rent for my parents a two-bedroomed flat on the ground floor in the same housing commission building that we lived in.

I was sitting in Mama's bedroom, looking out of the window watching the moon slowly disappear underneath a dark cloud. I always loved listening to Mama's myths and legends. I would sit and watch her making clothes and listen to her stories. She would sing songs of love and humanity and tell me stories of how to cope with life. I missed her melodious voice.

I moved towards Mama and watched her lips. Her voice had changed. She could no longer speak in full sentences. Every word was a big effort.

Our mother could hear us very well, though, even when we talked in low voices.

We talked in another room while the cassette player in her bedroom played cải lương, Vietnamese folk opera songs, loudly. We thought that she could not hear us, but we found out she knew everything we had said to each other if we spoke in Vietnamese. While she sat in her bedroom, she could tell who had opened the front door of her flat. She recognised our footsteps and the manner in which each of us unlocked the door to walk in. Not long after her arrival, Bé and I realised that she had a very good memory. She became our memory bank. Bé and I would tell her the events or the dates of our appointments. She always reminded us.

Tri walked in one day, soon after my parents' arrival, and said, quietly in English, that the doctors at the Royal Hobart Hospital diagnosed our mother with Motor Neurone Disease (MND).

I stared at him blankly.

Motor neurones are the nerve cells in the brain and spinal cord that control muscles. The brain has billions of neurones that control muscles so the body can function, and our hands and legs can move. When these neurones, or nerve cells, are weak, communication from the brain to the body parts weakens and ultimately is blocked. MND does not affect the brain.

Tri and Tuệ made enquiries with some people living on the mainland. They did everything they could to find out if there was any alternative way to heal our mother. They investigated Eastern medicines and they invited a monk and a nun from Melbourne to our home to see what they could do for her. No one had a cure.

Some kind volunteers suggested that we concentrate on improving the quality of our mother's life. The Housing Commission officers installed handrails in Mama's bathroom, and removed the steps along the footpath from the front door of her flat to the car park.

Whenever Tri sat with Mama, he would massage her feet and move her arms up and down. A few times a day, my father, or Tri, would slowly lift her up from her wheelchair. They would hold her up from behind and slowly walk with her from the door of the flat to the front door of the building, a distance of no more than ten metres. Papa and Tri hoped that Mama could strengthen her muscles and regain her movements.

I was tremendously sad watching her deteriorating, walking only a few steps with the assistance of Papa or Tri. Mama's ability to walk got worse. A year later, she could not stand up even with Papa's assistance. She was completely paralysed. She never complained.

From morning she waited for us to come home.

On the table in Mama's bedroom there were many boxes of cassette tapes that Tri and Tuệ had brought from Melbourne for her. Papa would play one tape after another. During the day, she would sit on her wheelchair and listen to whatever was on the cassette recorder: Nostalgic love songs about the three cities *Huế, Sài Gòn, Hà Nội* sung by Khánh Ly; *Dân Ca Ba Miền: Nam, Trung, Bắc* (folk songs from three regions South, Central, North) sung by Hoàng Oanh; *Bên Cầu Dệt Lụa* (Weaving by the Bridge) played by opera singer Thanh Nga; radio dramas with actresses Bạch Tuyết, Kim Cương and Ngọc Giàu, actors Thanh Sang, Minh Phụng, Thành Được and Hùng Cường, and the comedians Bảo Quốc and Tùng Lâm.

Mama said that she was content. After many years of separation she was finally living with her children again.

For all of her life, she had lived in war zones without any security, enduring the loss of her father at the age of eight and later facing the threat of losing her husband during the war with the North and her eldest son during the war between Việt Nam and the Khmer Rouge. She then lived through the fears of seeing her sons and daughters escape the country by small boats, in danger of facing the pirates and perils of ocean with only broken boats as means to travel.

After many years of separation from her children, finally she had found some measure of peace and togetherness.

All the horrors of the wars and their after-effects were now, for her, a distant memory.

Papa was Mama's primary carer. He received help from the MND Association of Tasmania and the Lions Club.

The founder of the MND Association of Tasmania told us that her husband had died of MND.

I was extremely sad. I could not accept that our mother would not live long. She was only forty-eight years old. Destiny could not be so cruel.

The MND association gave us a high-quality leather chair with wheels for Mama to sit on during the day and arranged for a large waterbed to be installed.

Volunteers from the association and the Lions Club assisted my parents. One lady came to help Mama to move her arms, and another to massage her. One man came to have a cup of tea with Papa and to play tennis with him when he was 'off duty'.

I appreciated the services my parents received. I thought often about the kindness of the MND Association and the Lions Club, of the volunteers who readily visited Mama at her home.

Because Mama could not turn herself, my siblings and I took turns to sleep with her so that we could turn her during the night to help her to sleep.

I slept with her one night a week and I sat with her whenever I was at home and did not have to study.

I watched helplessly as Mama suffered.

We understood each other and we both did our best to preserve the memory of the moments we were together and to prepare ourselves – she, for her eternal journey, and me, the strength to face the trials of life.

I loved Mama dearly but we never talked about our emotions. It was not a common practice within our culture or our family. I never said to her, 'I love you'.

I love her even more now as I reflect on her life.

Minh Hiền's mother, Quảng Ngãi, 1962.

Achievements

In the 1980s, I saw an article in the newspapers about Professor Stephen Hawking's life and work.

Professor Hawking had developed MND when he was a student at university. He then taught at Cambridge University and wrote books. He spoke with the assistance of a special keyboard on his computer. That made me want to study how to make a computer speak so that I could make one for Mama.

During summer vacation, January 1987, I found a twelve-week job with Telecom, the only telecommunication company in Australia at the time. Telecom had offices all over Australia and they were doing some engineering work in the Hobart office.

Computers were quite new at the time. To make a computer talk was a great achievement.

I volunteered for a project to develop an application for a blind operator.

The application would speak certain instructions to the operator when he moved his fingers over the keys on a special keyboard. Only the final testing of the application remained when my twelve-week period was over.

I graduated with an engineering degree with honours and obtained the second highest mark among all engineering students who graduated at the University of Tasmania that year.

Telecom was recruiting graduate engineers. I applied. The senior engineer called me into his office and in front of another male engineer said that he could not offer me the job because I graduated with honours.

Minh Hiền at her graduation, the University of Tasmania, April 1987.

A few days later, I found out that not only had he offered the job to one of my male classmates who had completed the degree with passing grades only, but he announced on television the news about a computer that talked to a blind operator.

All credit was given to that male classmate.

My hands were shaking as I watched this.

There was nothing I could do.

I turned and saw Mama sitting in a wheelchair motionless.

Her head had fallen forward. She was unable to lift it.

I took a deep breath and stood up.

I slowly lifted Mama's head up. I adjusted the scarf around her collar.

My mind was filled with thoughts: I needed a job to support my family. I could not leave Hobart.

My mother was in the last stages of MND. She could not talk in full sentences.

With great efforts, speaking one word at a time, she said, 'You do not need to work for people who do not appreciate education and devotion.'

Minh Hiền at her engineering graduation, the University of Tasmania, April 1987.

I applied for a scholarship to do a Master of Engineering Science by research. Due to my excellent academic achievements, I received the scholarship and was offered a research program at the University of Tasmania.

I wished to do my research in medical engineering but at the time the university did not offer that course. So I did my research in the new field of adaptive control: Non Parametric Model-Reference Adaptive-Control (NP-MRAC) that relies on estimating the shape of the Finite Impulse Response of the electrical plant and the controller. The NP-MRAC was studied both by digital simulation on the computer and by real-time hybrid-simulation on the signal processor.

Research into the application of processing chips was new in almost every field of science and engineering at the time. Researchers looked for innovative ways to apply the power of processors into their fields of study, whether it was engineering, computing or medicine. I was hoping to find a way to assist my mother. I studied full time for the master's degree while working as a tutor at the University of Tasmania.

During my studies, I got a job with the University of Tasmania in the Faculty of Medicine, located within the Hobart Royal Hospital.

I assisted a scientist, and head of the project, to develop a medical application, which we built with a doctor, a nurse and a computer programmer. The invention was a device that showed electronic signals generated from a patient's heart.

Doctors could use the device to assess the strength of someone's heart and to look for any warning signs. The aim was to assist them to diagnose any potential heart diseases early. I loved that job but at the time no research funds were available to continue the project.

Minh Hiền graduated with a Master of Engineering Science
The University of Tasmania, May 1990.

With a desire to rise above my disadvantaged background and to help others in need, I believed that education had the power to transform my family's lives.

Living in peaceful Australia, I have completed nine university qualifications in the fields of engineering, computing, accounting, management, writing and education while working. Whenever I found my career was undermined due to bad management, I re-educated myself and changed my career.

I have worked as an educator, a researcher, an engineer, an IT consultant, a systems accountant, a systems manager and a family business manager and owner in Hobart and Sydney. I have found that teaching was the most rewarding occupation. I have taught thousands of people from all walks of life. I have presented academic papers at international conferences and published research papers in international journals since 1988.

Articles about my achievements appeared in the *Bay-City Star* (1995), the *Newsprint Log* (1990), the *Sunday Tasmania* and the *Sunday Examiner* (1987), the *Mercury* and the *Examiner* (1983). Feature stories about me were published in *Who's Who in Tasmania* (2008), and the University of Tasmania Alumni Magazines (2017, 1993, and 1990).

Articles about Minh Hiền's achievements.

The highlight of my recent achievement was my short story, titled *My Mother*, shortlisted for the 2024 *Furphy Literary Award* (a prestigious Australian short story award). I am the recipient of multiple National Manuscript Development Programs: the Queensland Writers Centre (QWC) *Publishable* (2023 short-listed and 2022 long-listed), the QWC *Fellowship & Access Manuscript Development* (2021), the *Hardcopy* (2019) and the *Australian Society of Authors Mentorship* (2006). My application for the *Next Chapter* (a prestigious Australian literary award) was ranked in the top 10% of all 2019 submissions.

At the launch of *The Furphy Anthology 2024*, Melbourne, 21 November 2024.

At the *Furphy Literary Award,* Shepparton, 27 July 2024.

I had started creative writing twenty years ago when I wanted to write for Farshid and my brothers' daughters about the lives of my parents and what it was like to grow up during the wars and to leave my motherland on a dangerous journey. In 1981, when I arrived in Australia I learnt just enough English to enable me to study engineering and later to work in engineering, IT and accounting fields. In 2003, I enrolled for a Master of Arts in Creative Writing with a view of improving my English. The course broadened my knowledge of the English language beyond my expectation. I wrote and self-published *My Heritage: Vietnam fatherland motherland* in 2016.

Reading with my nieces at the *My Heritage* Book Launch, Sydney, September 2016.

I thought my nieces should learn our history and literature. Hence, I held functions inviting family, friends and the public to listen to my nieces reading extracts from *My Heritage*. All moneys collected from the sales of the books at these functions were donated to charity.

Charity Book Launch to support the work of the UNHCR, Hobart, December 2016.

Charity Book Talk to support the work of the UNHCR, Sydney, June 2017.

Charity Book Reading in memory of my mother on the 30th anniversary of her passing away to support to the *MND Association* of Tasmania, Glebe Town Hall, 21 June 2019.

To celebrate peace, I wrote *The Vietnamese Australians* series. The series documents for posterity what it was like to grow up during the wars and to leave my motherland on a dangerous journey to Australia. It presents a brief history of the Vietnamese Australians and the positive influences of the Vietnamese culture and customs on people in Australia over five decades.

The Vietnamese Australians Book Launch, Sydney, December 2023.

Photo courtesy of Dr Xuân (Susan) Đào.

The Vietnamese Australians Book Launch, Sydney, August 2024.

Love

Love gives life to the lifeless.

Love lights a flame in the heart that is cold.

Love brings hope to the hopeless and gladdens the hearts of the sorrowful.

In the world of existence there is indeed no greater power than the power of love.

Abdu'l-Bahá

If love and agreement are manifest in a single family,

that family will advance, become illumined and spiritual.

Abdu'l-Bahá

Love is the bridge between you and everything.

Rumi, Persian poet, 1207–1273

On the way to the writers' seminar, the *HardCopy*, Sydney Central Railway Station, Sep 2019.

During my undergraduate course, I learnt enough English to understand engineering subjects. After my graduation and when I was in the first year of my Master's degree, I enrolled in an evening English class.

I drove from our flat in Sandy Bay to the city along Davey Street then over the Tasman Bridge to Rosny College once a week for a three-hour class. My eldest brother Tri had bought me an old blue Toyota Cressida from the money I had earned working during summers.

One evening during a coffee break, a man approached me from behind.

As I turned my head towards his direction, he said, 'You are an engineer.'

I smiled. 'I am not sure about that.'

'You are studying for a Master's degree.'

'Yes,' I turned and walked towards the stairs.

'May I have your phone number?' He asked in a very soft voice.

I halted my steps and turned my head towards him. I saw that he held a pen in one hand and a notepad in another, ready to write. He wore dark brown pants and a lighter brown coloured jumper over a white shirt and tie, also in brown.

I immediately recognised who he was as he was the only student in the English class who had a moustache. During the introduction session at the beginning of the course he had said to the class that he was Persian and he worked as an engineer. He looked more like an Italian than an Iranian. I had known a few refugees from Iran who were studying at university. I had also met many Persians who were Bé's classmates and one of my female friends from university was Persian so I felt comfortable to tell him my phone number at university.

That evening happened to be the last evening I attended my English class. As the term was progressing, I got more involved in my Master's studies and in teaching undergraduate students. And I would have had to spend a lot of time doing the weekly English assignments and reading the required literature so I stopped studying English.

A few months later, I received a phone call from a man who said he had met me at the English class. He asked if he could see me.

'What do you want to see me for?' I asked.

He paused for a moment then said, 'I am considering further studies. I want to ask your opinion about an academic paper and postgraduate studies.'

'What is the academic paper about?'

'Power engineering'

By nature I would help all those who approached me for help. Power engineering was not something I was interested in even though I got a distinction for that subject during my undergraduate course. I agreed to meet him to talk about the paper he was reading and about what it means to do postgraduate studies.

'Okay then,' I said. 'I can meet you at the engineering building.'

I told him my room number and how to find it.

I shared a large room with Chandrani who came from Sri Lanka to study a Master's degree in communications. Chandrani was in the room when he arrived.

We talked a little then he left.

He rang me again not long after that. Chandrani answered the phone. She put her hand over the phone, turned around and stared at me.

'For you,' she said with a big smile, 'the engineer from your English class.'

'I don't know his name,' I said. 'Can you ask him?'

'What is your name?' Chandrani asked. 'How do you spell it?'

Chandrani wrote F A R S H I D on a piece of paper as I read over her shoulder. She then passed the phone to me.

'What do you do at lunch time?' Farshid asked.

'I eat my lunch.' I replied.

Silence on the other side.

This time he asked if he could meet me for a coffee.

We drove to a café in Sandy Bay, a short drive from the university. He showed me the academic paper. We talked a little about it. Then we talked about postgraduate studies and a little bit about life in general.

I paid for his coffee.

I never let a stranger, especially a man, pay for my coffee because I do not want to owe anyone anything. It did not occur to me that Farshid interpreted my action differently, that I wanted to see him again. Because now he had another excuse to re-visit me as he now owed me a coffee!

And so for the next few months he would contact me again, and again, and again for a coffee. He was a coffee addict.

On my twenty-fifth birthday I wore my purple blouse, embroidered with eight large sunflowers, which Mama had made for me six years earlier. When I walked outside, over my favourite blouse I wore a purple leather jacket which my eldest brother Tri gave me for my previous birthday. It felt really good to still fit well in my favourite sunflowers blouse.

I spent all day making hundreds of Vietnamese spring-rolls. I rarely celebrated my birthday. But this was a special occasion as I had invited Farshid and his parents to attend my birthday at my parents' flat.

My parents and my elder brothers were shocked.

I had met many of my brothers' friends. I had received them as friends and so I expected the same with Farshid. The elders in my family did not share my innocent thoughts.

I was twenty-five years old but for my parents I was still a seventeen-year-old girl, who had left their home in Saigon to go abroad to study.

Time had stood still for them and they had forgotten that I was now a postgraduate student. And according to Tri my understanding of men was no more than a twelve-year-old Australian girl's.

The Vietnamese boys could come to our home any time because they were my brothers' friends. But Farshid could not.

And I did not invite Farshid alone either. I invited him and his parents. So it was natural that my parents were concerned. My parents gave Tri the task of telling me right from wrong.

Tri told me the concerns of my parents.

'Don't worry,' I said. 'I won't invite Farshid and his parents to our home again.'

Well, that did not mean that I did not meet Farshid and his parents at his home. I did not tell Tri that but he knew I would meet Farshid elsewhere.

I had met Farshid at the university and at a coffee shop a few times before I invited him to have a dinner at my parents' home on my birthday.

We had many conversations about life in general. I shared many of his views about life. I wanted to know him better.

My parents did not want me to make friends with any men from other countries. They wanted me to marry a Vietnamese man. They were worried about cultural differences.

On the other hand, I had witnessed many dysfunctional Vietnamese married couples, so I never thought that husband and wife had to be from the same culture.

To me, it is important that husband and wife share the same principles and values in life.

I was brought up with the understanding that marriage is for life and at that time there was no Vietnamese man in Hobart that I could consider living with for the rest of my life.

It took me a few months to convince Mama to receive Farshid again at her flat.

I said to Mama, 'Farshid does not drink. He does not smoke. He looks after his parents. He is a gentleman. He works as an engineer at the Hydro.'

Mama listened carefully then said, 'But you are studying for a Master's degree and he does not have a Master's degree.'

I smiled. I knew why Mama said that. In her view, which was also the same view of many people of her generation, women should not be too clever. She believed that for a marriage to last the husband must be more educated than the wife.

'In Australia it does not matter,' I said. 'He finished his engineering studies. Now he works. If he studies now, he will not have enough money to pay for household expenses. He can do more study later.'

Mama asked me more about Farshid's background.

I told her that he used to live in Melbourne. Before that he lived in India for more than ten years. He left Iran for India when he was a child.

Mama was sick and could not talk in full sentences but what I could make out from the few words she uttered was that she wanted to know if he had a wife in India and another one in Melbourne!

Papa was there. He explained to me that Mama had met Iranians and Indians when she had a dress-making shop in Saigon. She knew about Iranian men.

'An Iranian man could marry four or five wives,' said Papa. 'They treat their wives as their property. There is no equality between men and women.'

I was surprised at Papa's explanation and I didn't know that Mama had met Iranians before.

I held Mama's hands and looked at the hands that had worked very hard for the education of her own six children, two adopted children, two brothers, one sister, one half-sister and for financially supporting her extended family while she was able to.

Mama lost her father when she was in grade three. She never went back to school after his death. Bound by family tradition, she had worked selflessly to support her siblings so that they could continue going to school and could graduate from university.

She was a dressmaker all her life.

She had turned fabric into beautiful *áo dài* (traditional Vietnamese dress) and dresses for tens of thousands of women and children to wear in homes, schools, offices, temples, churches long before I was born, and while I was living in Hobart she was still making them and teaching others how to sew. The only time of the year she would rest was Tết.

While I was living in Hobart and she was in Saigon, she made me more beautiful, colourful-embroidered blouses and sent them, one by one, in a brown-paper envelope.

She made me purple, red and blue blouses and a red jumper. She made me a dark blue blouse embroidered with blue sunflowers. She made me a red blouse with red roses delicately strung as a garland in the shape of the heart.

Now as I held her hands up to my face, my mind's eye saw:

Seven colours she picks: purple, gold, red, blue, orange, green, deep blue,

Through seven tiny eyes, steadily her hand guides,

The pure white fabric, firmly she grips, little by little leaving behind a tiny trace,

Up and down her hands move, seven days, seven nights, weeks,

Patiently she repeats: Áo dài, people, flower, sky, sun, bamboo, ocean,

Splendid art she creates,

Royalty, loyalty, love, hope, honesty, tenacity, generosity, she relates.

I looked into Mama's eyes.

'If that is the cause of your worry for me then you should not be worried at all. Farshid is a Baha'i. He is a religious man. The Baha'i Faith does not allow such things to happen.'

A few months later Farshid proposed and I said, 'My parents have to approve.'

'Of course,' he said. 'The Baha'i Faith requires the approval of both biological parents.'

I was surprised but I was pleased because the more I get to know Farshid and his Baha'i Faith, the more I realised that we hold the same values.

In my office during my research for a *Master of Engineering Science*, 1988

Farshid shaved his moustache before Mama accepted him as her son-in-law because she said that she did not like a man with a moustache. It had reminded her of Rhett Butler in the *Gone with the Wind* movie, who had frequently declared that he was no gentleman and he had no honour.

One day when Farshid stopped by at my room at the University of Tasmania, I gave him a bookmark which I had made that afternoon.

On a piece of white paper, I drew a picture of a house with two people outside and the words: *If you love me as I love you, even death cannot part us two.*

When we married, I vowed to stay with my husband for the rest of my life. That's how I was brought up. And as long as my mother was living, my husband would have to make her happy by following certain Vietnamese customs, irrespective of his nationality. He would not have to follow every custom as I, myself, had left many customs behind when I stepped into the wooden boat in 1981. But some customs, I had always kept, and one of those customs was to consult with Mama to get her approval about the details of our engagement and marriage celebrations.

We got engaged in January of the Year of the Dragon 1989.

I was my parents' first daughter but I was the third one in the family. Yet I was the first one to get engaged.

Farshid and I organised almost everything ourselves and everything was approved by Mama. We celebrated at an Asian restaurant in Kingston. There was neither a Vietnamese nor a Persian restaurant in Hobart at the time.

Our engagement, January of the *Year of the Dragon* 1989.

Six months after our engagement, one evening, Farshid and I stopped at a restaurant to buy takeaway for dinner.

We planned to spend the evening discussing with Mama, who was admitted into hospital during the weekend, how to celebrate my marriage.

We were going to discuss my wedding dress.

When I reached the hospital, I saw the curtain was drawn and I heard my father weeping.

I entered the room quietly.

I sat on a chair beside Mama's bed and held one of her hands.

Tears welled up in my eyes, flowed over my face and dropped on my hands.

Mama had stopped breathing at about the time I was waiting for the takeaway.

She had left this earth without saying goodbye.

I recall Mama's smile from the night before.

The evening of 20 June 1989, I had sat a long time with her. We talked about our plans for the marriage ceremony.

I did not know then that would be my last evening with Mama.

As I was about to leave the hospital that night I leaned over and touched her hands, she gave me the most beautiful smile I ever saw.

Her beautiful smile is imprinted on my mind forever.

That evening, as I watched Mama's last smile, standing behind me was Farshid.

I do not know what was in her mind.

Perhaps she smiled for our future happiness together.

Perhaps she smiled, satisfied that I had found a handsome and caring husband whom she could trust to live with her daughter for the rest of her life.

I know, though, that is how she wanted me to remember her - her lovely smile, not her weak body.

I did not know at the time that the love in my mother's smile would never leave my memory.

The love in her smile has given me the courage to face the difficulties that life has thrown at me.

At home in Blackmans Bay, Tasmania, September of the *Year of the Snake* 1989.

Tenacity

Let me tell you the secret that has led me to my goal.

My strength lies solely in my tenacity.

Louis Pasteur, French microbiologist, 1822–1895

Many of life's failures are people who did not realize

how close they were to success when they gave up.

Thomas A. Edison, American inventor and businessman, 1847–1931

With my father at my grandparents' house in Tiên Am, Vĩnh Bảo, Hải Phòng 2007.

This was the first brick house in our ancestral village. My grandparent's house in the village was designed by my grandfather and built by local builders from the money that was secretly saved by my grandmother.

My village was famous for *thuốc lào* (Vietnamese tobacco). My grandfather made regular trips to Vinh to sell thuốc lào from the village. He always made good money from those trips but he also loved to buy nice things. He often brought home expensive hand-painted porcelain plates, rare flowers and rare fruits. When one day my grandfather brought home a peacock and a peahen instead of cash, my grandmother told him to let her go instead of him. This surprised everyone in the village because in those days village women never went anywhere beyond their district market.

To cut the costs, my grandmother hired a sail boat to take her tobacco from her local beach to Bến Thủy wharf in Nghệ An, three hundred kilometres away from home, in the Gulf of Tokin. She never bought anything, just hid the profit. Three-and-a-half years after her first business trip, she gave my grandfather a bag of money and gold leaves and said 'for you to decorate our houses for the Tết celebration of The Year of The Dragon 1940.'

With that large bagful of money, my grandfather replaced the thatched roofs of their two wooden cottages with tile. Then he engaged an architect to design an elevated brick house to be located at the centre, of the courtyard, with *nhà ba giang*, (Vietnamese traditional cottage), on the left, and on right, the two-storey cottage. He designed the new home as a blend of French and traditional Vietnamese architectural design. There were two large windows on each side, with wooden louvres which opened outwardly. All doors and windows were painted deep blue.

I never met my grandmother, but when I met my father's younger brother in May 1975, he said, 'you strikingly resemble your grandmother in features and in character!'

In 1981, when my father tried to convince me to leave Việt Nam in a small fishing boat, he said, 'Your grandmother used to go to sea in a sail boat! Be strong like her!'

Thuốc lào in my ancestral village, Tiên Am, Vĩnh Bảo, Hải Phòng 2007.

Tenacity is a trait in my family.

Tenacity and indomitable faith have assisted me in performing well in all my positions at work.

My childhood and my refugee experiences have made me resilient.

My parents worked extremely hard to bring us up during the war, to survive the harsh life during the late 1970s. By watching how my parents dealt with difficulties, I have learnt to be patient and to plan well ahead of time in all circumstances.

I have never met my father's father, but, I have heard many inspirational stories about him.

My grandfather's parents were very poor, however, my grandfather loved learning and through learning he had built himself up to the highest level of literary knowledge in our ancestral village. He was the last *Ông Hội* (Chief of Cultural Activities) of our ancestral village.

My grandparents worked very hard to save money to send my father to the city of Vinh to study. When Việt Nam was under French rule, only very rich people could afford to pay for their son's education. During those times, for the Vietnamese living in the North and Central regions Vinh came third after Hà Nội and the Royal City Húê in terms of education and after Hà Nội and Hải Phòng in terms of commerce. But in those years Hà Nội was an exclusive area for European residents and the Royal City Húê was for the sons of the rich mandarins. So for boys from villages, like my father, and middle-class Vietnamese, Collège Vinh was the best. It was the largest establishment in the whole province.

My father was the first from his village to travel some three hundred kilometres for a primary education. He was thirteen and was about to re-start the fourth grade, which was the first grade in a French school. Four decades later, he would be the first - and the only - man from his village to send me, his seventeen-year-old daughter all the way from Sài Gòn to Hobart for my education.

My brothers and I made many attempts to leave Việt Nam. Unfortunately, people kept cheating my parents. We were lucky that we were not caught and jailed. The loss of gold did not deter my tenacious father.

Every time Papa failed, he recalled his father's voice. Papa's father taught my father to use both *Trí* and *Thiện* (head and heart) when facing difficulties.

Regarding Trí, Papa was very careful in his planning. He was aware of the risk at sea. He did not want to take chances by relying on others to organise, and so he became part of the organising group. He made sure he or his trusted friends inspected everything. Many things had to be taken care of: the boat, food, water, first aid, petrol, engines, drivers, engineers, doctors, group leaders, the place and time of departure, transport to the village, the villagers' willingness to house the fugitives, phases of the moon, people's emotions and clothing.

Regarding Thiện, Papa promised himself to organise for all those friends and relatives to whom he was in debt to leave Việt Nam, or to pay them for the losses they suffered, even if it was not his fault. After a few failures, the amount of gold Papa lost was so great that it took my brothers and I many years to pay his debt. A decade later, Farshid and I made the final payment to a man whom Papa felt he was obliged to pay even though we did not agree that Papa owed the man any money.

Remembering my grandfather's philosophy, Papa had named me *Minh Hiền*.

'Minh and Hiền are the feminine words for Trí and Thiện,' Papa said.

In English, the meaning of my name is 'one should use both head and heart'.

Using my head means I like learning. Using my heart means I like helping others by teaching them what I know and to help them to progress. Learning and teaching have helped me to overcome many difficulties. I began to teach when I was in junior high school. While I was working as a Systems Accountant at a university in Sydney, I taught accounting students during lunch breaks and after I finished my normal working hours.

In November 2017, Farshid and I presented a paper about online teaching at an IT international conference held at the Quảng Nam University in Tam Kỳ, Việt Nam. While we were in Tam Kỳ there was a flood that stopped us from going to our next destination, so we stayed in Tam Kỳ for ten more days. This provided us with an opportunity to teach English to students at the Quảng Nam University.

November 2017, presenting a paper at Quảng Nam University, Tam Kỳ, Việt Nam.

A few weeks later we delivered an online teaching course from Australia to the second-year students and Farshid conducted surveys for his PhD project. Our teaching and learning were purely voluntary.

Seven months later, I was diagnosed with breast cancer. While the chemotherapy drugs were drop-by-drop entering into my veins, I saw on Facebook that my online students' town was under water. The water had risen so high that my students could not go to university. I posted messages encouraging them to spend time studying with me while they could not attend their normal classes. I posted activities for them to study and commented on their posts. I encouraged them to learn English in teams and to support each other during times of difficulty.

Since then we have taught many students from rural areas of Việt Nam online.

Our four courses require the students to study every day for a period of nine weeks each course. Some students have studied with us every year for four years from their first year until their final year at their university. We teach them English using reflective practice. We have activities that help students to develop their critical thinking and encourage them to be tenacious.

Home

My home is the home of peace.

My home is the home of joy and delight.

My home is the home of laughter and exultation.

Whosoever enters through the portals of this home,

must go out with gladsome heart.

This is the home of light; whosoever enters here must become illumined.

Abdu'l-Bahá, Star of the West, Volume 5, p. 40.

A few years after marriage, we bought a four-bedroomed home with a large living space on the five acres of land in Albion Heights, Kingston, Tasmania, which was surrounded by the green landscape and facing the blue ocean. We wanted our children to have room to grow with nature. Our home has plenty of wildlife and the air is pure. We love this place.

At home in Albion Heights, Kingston, 1992.

Six years after our marriage we still had no children. Doctors found nothing wrong with either of us. Because there was nothing wrong, my GP advised us to try IVF.

After three failed attempts at IVF in Hobart, I wanted to move to the mainland to follow my dreams. Before leaving Hobart, I studied for a Master of Commerce for one year which would normally take one-and-a-half years to complete.

Studying for a Master of Commerce at home in Albion Heights, Kingston, 1997.

We left Hobart in 1998.

In Sydney, we both got full time jobs very quickly. So we rented out our house in Albion Heights until the Covid-19 pandemic.

Now, we keep our Albion Heights home for creativity and hospitality activities. We visit whenever we can. Sitting behind our desks, we can look at nature through full-length glass windows. We feel peaceful, calm and free.

Some visitors to our home in Albion Heights, Kingston, February 2022.

Birds like our home in Albion Heights, Kingston, January 2022.

Albion Heights, Kingston, May 2022.

Albion Heights, Kingston, April 2022.

Albion Heights, Kingston, May 2022.

Albion Heights, Kingston, May 2022.

In our Albion Heights home, we entertain friends and families from Sydney and Hobart.

With Margaret Eldridge (my English teacher since the day I arrived in Hobart in 1981),
Albion Heights, May 2023.

Celebrating my great-nephew's birthday with his family from Sydney and Việt Nam
Albion Heights, January 2023.

In Sydney we worked long hours in IT, accounting and teaching and we managed to buy our own homes.

At our first Sydney home, July 2022.

At our second Sydney home, *Tết*, the first day of the Year of the Dragon 2024.

Education in Việt Nam starts at home when children speak their first word.

A child learns morality and paying respect to elders by learning subtle ways of expressing gratitude and expressing respect for elders.

For example, the word "you" can be any one of the following words: mình, em, anh, chị, bạn, nhỏ, mi, mày, đồng chí, nhà mình, con, cháu, cụ, ông, bà, thầy, cô, chú, thím, dì, cậu, mợ, dượng, o, mệ, mụ, bác, u, bu, me, mẹ, má, mạ, ba, bố, cha, tiá, má nó, ba nó, ông xã, bà xã etc. The correct word depends on whom one is speaking to and what their relationship is, on sentiment, age, regional accent, sex, social status, educational background, etc.

Myths and legends have played a great part in Vietnamese daily lives, especially for the older generation. Their ways of living have sprung from a society with deep roots in Ancestor Worship, Buddhism and Confucianism.

Proverbs and poems were a common way of speaking among the people of my parents' and elders' generations who cared passionately for their ancestral lands.

Being Vietnamese, I believe that when my grandparents and my mother pass away, they do not just disappear; they continue to watch over me. Hence, like most Vietnamese, I have a family altar in my home wherever I am living. Traditionally we, Vietnamese, do not celebrate our birthdays. Instead we hold special feasts on the anniversary of our loved ones' passing away, ngày giỗ.

Minh Hiền's altar table in Sydney, Tết, the first day of the Year of the Buffalo 2021.

Youth

Mount Wellington, Hobart, Tasmania, July 1981.

All Vietnamese girls of my generation and earlier learned needle-work at school and at home from a very young age as part of our education. We learned to embroider handkerchiefs, clothes and items for people we loved or cared for. We made clothes for our family and ourselves to wear.

When I was aged ten, I learned embroidery at school. At age thirteen, I taught other girls embroidery at home. Embroidery has influenced my decisions and actions in my adult life.

When I married, I made embroidery items and hung them on the wall to celebrate our marriage. I made baby clothes and embroidered them.

When I completed a Master of Engineering Science, I bought a long red dress and I embroidered on it for wearing at my graduation ceremony. Remembering my mother and her explanations of how the dress shows a woman's character, I chose a red colour for my love of my mother and for prosperity as I was looking into a bright future after completing a Master degree in engineering. I embroidered *Chim Phượng Hoàng* (a phoenix) on the left front as the phoenix is a mythical bird that symbolises grace, nobility, virtue, pride, survival.

According to the Vietnamese myth, Chim Phượng Hoàng rose from the ashes, hence it also symbolises rebirth and she normally hides herself in times of trouble then reappears at a calm and prosperous time. Thus the phoenix also symbolises peace.

At home in my embroidered dress and my embroidered item on the wall.
Blackmans Bay, Tasmania, 1990.

I was eighteen when I arrived in Hobart.

A few months after my arrival, my eldest brother Tri handed me a brown-paper envelope addressed to me.

'What's inside?' I asked nervously as I felt its softness.

'Open it,' Tri said. 'It's from mother.' He was curious and wanted me to hurry up.

When I touched the silken purple, I saw my mother bending her head over a piece of fabric, holding it carefully with her left hand while up and down her right hand moved, pulling a tiny needle with a long thread, little by little leaving a small trace of red, orange, yellow, green. My mother had made me a new blouse.

I spread the blouse on my bed and ran my fingers over the silken threads. It had short puff sleeves and a round neck. There were eight large sunflowers, eight buds and fourteen green leaves. Each flower was centred with numerous seeds of red, surrounded by large petals in bright orange and shining yellow.

I heard Mama's melodious voice from the other side of the Pacific Ocean:

> *Green is the colour of tenacity,*
>
> *Purple is the colour of royalty and nobility,*
>
> *Red is the colour of the five-fingered flower – the flower of love,*
>
> *Orange is the colour of the sun – the sun of honesty,*
>
> *Yellow is the colour of gold – gold for people – the people of loyalty,*
>
> *Be like the sunflower – always turn towards the sun -*
>
> *the sun of truth, loyalty and honesty.*

'Yes, mother,' I said as I touched the sunflowers. My fingers rested on a large leaf and thought, green for the bamboo – the bamboo of tenacity.

As I touched the threads I decided I would only wear my sunflower blouse on special occasions so that I could preserve its beauty forever.

I had watched my mother making clothes since I was born. Whenever she made a new blouse or a new áo dài, the Vietnamese traditional dress, she would explain why she chose certain colours, why she made certain styles and why they looked good on me.

A beautifully made áo dài with embroidery is a piece of art that shows the core characteristics of the woman who wears it. An áo dài with embroidery shows that a woman of the twentieth century is not just an obedient daughter, a faithful wife, a devoted mother, but also a gracious and dignified individual who not only has the four traditional virtues of

Hobart, 1988.

Công, Dung, Ngôn and *Hạnh* (diligence, elegance, proper speech and good behaviour) but also works professionally to support her family.

At home in Albion Heights in 1993.

When I arrived in Australia, the sole endeavour I made at the time was to get a university qualification because that was what my parents wanted and that was the reason they had sent me to Australia. I wanted to enrol for Matriculation the following year in March.

I had eight months to learn English. I had studied English as a subject for a few years at high school. After 30 April 1975, English was discouraged and I never had a chance to practise English with Westerners until I was in the refugee camp.

In Hobart, I had no friends to talk to and there were no English classes for a few weeks after I arrived. So Tri asked Sister Anne, a Catholic nun, whom he met through his job, to teach me English at home while I was waiting for a proper English class.

Sister Anne was very tall, quite large and a mature-aged woman. She visited refugees at their homes, talked to them and taught them simple English. She saw me once a week for about an hour. She gave me a picture dictionary. She read and I repeated after her. Tri and Tuệ had a few English books, I also read from those books with Sister Anne. I wrote a short piece every week and she corrected my usage of words, grammar and spelling mistakes. I wrote English on a notepad, which I tied together with an old shoelace to make a note book. I still keep that note book.

A few weeks later I attended a formal English class. My teacher, Mrs Margaret Eldridge, was a well-built and tall English woman with a caring face. Considering that I was a tiny girl, she looked like a giant. She had an equally big and kind heart, as I found out later. She was the teacher-in-charge of the English language program at Mount St Canice Migrant Hostel. Most of the Vietnamese refugees who first came to Hobart lived there. She inspired confidence in me to learn English. After the ten-week course with her, I studied English at evening classes for a few weeks at the Adult Migrant Education Centre in a building next to the State Library.

It was a Thursday in November 1981, when Tri came back from work and said, 'Do you want to teach?'

'Teach whom?' I asked.

'The head of the Migrant Resource Centre (MRC), Mrs Elizabeth Liew, asked me if I knew someone who could teach high school students Mathematics and Science. I could not think of anyone better than you.'

I had shown my studious nature since I was at primary school. When I was in fifth grade, I often came to Tri with lots of questions. One day, he gave me a very thick book and said that the answers to my questions were in the book. When I asked him for the page number, he said he did not remember which page it was. He thought that would keep me away from him for a few weeks! However a few days later I told him the answers and that I had finished reading the whole book.

'Think about it,' Tri said. 'She wants the answer by the end of this week before she looks for someone else.'

'Do you think I can do it?' I asked. 'I have been in Australia for only four months and I have only finished a short course of English.'

'I do not have any doubt about your ability to teach,' said Tri. 'They are refugee students. Many are Vietnamese. Some are East Europeans. I will borrow books from the library for you to prepare lessons.'

'Ok. I will do it,' I said.

Then for the following two months, to save money on bus fares, I cycled to the State Library on Tri's yellow bike. When I sat on his bike, my arms were straight and my shoulders leaned forward towards the handles. There was no basket in the front and no rack at the back for me to put my bag. It had the triangle frame; the top tube was horizontal, parallel to the ground, holding the seat and the handles together. I rested my bag against the top tube while gripping firmly on the bag handles with my left hand while riding. I wore no helmet. My waist-length black hair was flowing freely in the gentle wind of summer as I rode along Giblin Street, turned right to Augusta Road passing Calvary Hospital, and turned right to Elizabeth Street. I had no fear of cars and buses that lined up behind me. The steep hills along some parts of the road and the sharp curve of Elizabeth

Street and the stream of cars behind and in-front of me did not discourage me. I was young, fit and I had been riding a bicycle along busy streets in Saigon since I was ten years old.

I had always loved the library atmosphere. My spirits lifted as I walked along a row of bookshelves. From one row to another, I picked up high school physics, chemistry and mathematics books. I glanced through them then carried them to a large table and spread them out. To save money on photocopying, I wrote passages extracted from the books into my notebook. I sat for hours reading and writing. I turned page after page as I wrote lessons which I imagined that someone a few years younger than me would want to learn. I enjoyed preparing lessons for the students and I felt good about teaching young people.

It was school holidays. Elizabeth College allowed the MRC to use their classrooms. It was a beautiful summer. I carried my notebooks in my bag and walked with seven young people, aged between thirteen and sixteen, from the MRC at 222 Elizabeth Street to Elizabeth College. We crossed at the traffic lights then walked through a large courtyard. We climbed the wide stairways then turned into a large room with a high ceiling. There were rows of desks and benches facing two large green boards on the wall. In a corner there was a large desk.

The young people sat on the first two wooden benches while I stood on the other side of the wooden desk on the first row. I laid down my notebooks and asked them what they wanted to learn. They spoke to each other in their own languages for a few minutes then a Polish girl, about fifteen years old, asked me what mathematics in Australia is like.

I showed her the lessons that I had written in my notebook from the State library.

She read it carefully then looked up and smiled.

'Same, same,' she said as she passed my notebook to her friend.

The young people in the second row came over to my side and peered into my handwritten notebook. The Vietnamese boys asked me many questions in Vietnamese.

I explained to them in English that no matter where they came from mathematics was the same.

Their eyes were sparkling.

I smiled. Then I glanced at all the students and said slowly, 'the very famous German Mathematician, David Hilbert, had said "Mathematics knows no races or geographic boundaries; for mathematics, the cultural world is one country".'

I was not sure if their English was adequate to understand, so I asked, 'Do you understand what I said?'

The Polish girls shook their heads.

The Vietnamese boys asked me in Vietnamese, 'What does that mean?'

I walked to the board, picked up a piece of white chalk and wrote on the green board the sentence then I told them to check the new words in their dictionary.

They got together in groups, turned the pages of their pocket dictionary and read.

After a few minutes, they all looked up at me and smiled.

My spirits were lifted.

I had just passed my first day of teaching Mathematics in Australia.

I got paid for the hours I taught.

The payment was not much for an Australian, but it was quite a big sum for a refugee who had just arrived. I saved every dollar which I earned to send to my parents.

Mrs Liew said that the refugee young people loved learning from me. I got a teaching job again the following two summers. Later, I found out that Mrs Liew received some money from the government for a Christmas party but she baked cakes at home for the party and put most of the money aside to pay for tutors to teach refugees rather than spending all the money on cakes and drink. I was impressed.

At eighteen, I had one clear aim which was that I would go to university to study for an engineering degree so that I could work in my chosen profession and would lead a useful and independent life. The requirements to get to university were that I had to pass all six level-three Matriculation subjects which normally took two years to complete.

'You can enrol for five subjects,' my elder brother Tuệ said in an enthusiastic voice. 'You can attend classes for two mathematics subjects, two physics subjects and a chemistry subject. You can study another mathematics subject on your own without enrolment, at the end of the year you can sit for six examinations.'

Tuệ did not have any doubt that I would complete six subjects in one year, even though he himself did only four subjects. He was two years older than I and had come to Hobart eighteen months before me. As a mature-age student he was allowed to go to university when he passed four level-three matriculation subjects. For the mathematics subject in which I did not enrol, I could use his notes to study, and if needed, I could enrol in an evening class that ran for mature adults. With Tuệ's encouragement, I enrolled for five level-three subjects but planned to matriculate with six level-three subjects at the end of that year.

Mrs Sue Baker-Finch taught me Physics and Advanced Physics subjects. She also voluntarily taught English lessons to non-English speaking students, like me, during lunch breaks. She asked me how old I was and where I lived. I was almost nineteen years old at the time. She asked me whether I could baby sit her one-year-old daughter. She explained to me what a babysitter does. She said if I agreed she would ask her husband to come and pick me up from my home and drive me to their place in Lenah Valley. Of course, I agreed because in Việt Nam it was a privilege to be asked by your teachers to come to their home. So throughout that year, while I was at Hobart Matriculation College, whenever Mrs Baker-Finch and her husband went out, either he or she would come and take me to their home. I would eat dinner there with ice-cream for dessert, which was a luxury for me. I would watch her feeding her baby daughter. Then I would say good night to the baby and I would study in her nice comfortable lounge room until she and her husband came home about three hours later.

I found the babysitting service arrangement totally strange.

I did not want to take my teacher's money as I believed that I did nothing. I was fed a good meal and then I studied just as if I was at my own home. But she insisted that I take the money. I did not know how to explain to her that I could not accept money for doing my study in her home. So, I took the money but I did not spend it. At the end of the year after my examinations were all over, I bought a dress for the baby and embroidered a beautiful picture of a child standing in a garden on her dress. But by the time I finished the embroidery, the baby had grown up and the dress became a blouse – I did not know that babies grew so fast! Till this day I have treasured the memories of my babysitting time and my hours of embroidering the dress for my Physics teacher's daughter.

I enjoyed embroidery and made quite a few pieces for family and friends during holidays. I embroidered a blouse for my sister for her to wear on her eleventh birthday. I embroidered Việt Võ logo on the uniforms of my brother's Martial Art students.

In December 1982, I passed six Matriculation subjects with very high marks.

I got the highest mark among the Tasmanian Matriculation students for the Advanced Mathematics subject. I was among the top five in the State. I achieved my goal and I had my freedom to study for an Electrical Engineering degree. I felt lucky that I could study for my chosen profession and gain work experience in my adopted country where I would live a life of freedom and peace.

On Wednesday 12 January 1983, when I was sitting in the library of the MRC, a journalist and a cameraman from the Mercury newspaper came to interview me. My picture appeared on the front page of the Mercury two days later.

The journalist wrote a nice article and I loved the photo in the paper, but the Mercury did not print the journalist and the photographer's names. I wish I knew who they were.

A few weeks later, another journalist and another photographer came to the MRC to interview me and to take my photo. A full length article about me and my achievements was printed and circulated throughout Tasmania by the Examiner newspaper.

Receiving an award for the highest mark for the Advanced Mathematics subject among the Tasmanian Matriculation students, Hobart Matriculation College, 1983.

Mind

Your Mind is a powerful thing.

When you filter it with positive thoughts, your life will start to change.

We are shaped by our thoughts; we become what we think.

When the mind is pure, joy follows like a shadow that never leaves.

Buddha

A cheerful heart is good medicine,

but a crushed spirit dries up the bones.

The Bible, the Book of Proverbs 17:23

Ships don't sink because of the water around them.

Ships sink because of the water that gets in them.

Don't let what's happening around you

get inside you and weigh you down.

Author Unknown

Đường không khó vì ngăn sông cách núi,

Mà chỉ khó vì lòng người ngại núi e sông.

The road is not made difficult by rivers and mountains,

But by the heart that is scared of the mountains and rivers.

Hữu chí cánh thành.

Those who have willpower will succeed.

Vietnamese Proverbs

At the shrine of the Bab, Israel, 1996.

The Year of the Dog, 2018, Farshid turned sixty.

He was doing his PhD in human-computer interaction at the university where I used to work for ten years. Since he started doing his Masters, I had co-authored and co-presented papers with him about the influences of personality on cognition and learning.

He did not want to travel to Japan to present a paper at the Pacific Asia Conference on Information Systems, one of the leading conferences on IT, because he had heard that according to the Vietnamese horoscope it would be a difficult year for us.

We had seen terrible things happened to men who turned sixty. My father lost my mother when he was sixty. Farshid's adopted Vietnamese father also lost his wife when he was sixty.

'Don't be superstitious,' I said. 'You have worked so hard for your PhD and presenting papers is part of your PhD's requirements.'

We were on our way to Yokohama for the conference when he noticed a small lump in my breast.

At the Pacific Asia Conference on Information Systems (PACIS), Yokohama, Japan, 2018.

One month after we returned from Japan, I was resting in bed when Farshid told me that his supervisor did not like the work-in-progress draft version of his paper that he planned to submit to the premier International Conference on Software Engineering (ICSE).

I asked him to show it to me. He passed me his laptop.

'I agree with her,' I said after I read his draft paper. 'What you have written so far can lead to a good paper, but it does not suit the ICSE 2019 conference theme.'

I looked up from his laptop. 'What have you done about the peer review? I thought you were working on that.'

'I did, but I have not got far with it,' Farshid said. 'I fail.' He suddenly raised his voice. 'I can't get my head around it. I haven't been able to do it ...'

He went on and on in a sad and disappointed voice for a while.

I knew what he had gone through and so I let him pour out the sadness that was rising from his heart. I could see that he was on the verge of depression.

It had been the worst year of our life: my cancer; my court case with my employer for my workplace rights; the death of his dearest and much loved brother the previous month; the bleak prospect of finding any future employment for either of us; the slow progress of his PhD; the remote attitudes of his supervisors; the lack of budget allocated to his PhD project by the university and by the IT department; the isolation from others at the university; the negative treatment towards him from some people working at the university; the list went on and on.

I stayed silent while he spoke.

The thick curtains blocked the light of the sun from entering our bedroom window.

The room was dark. Our moods were matched with our surroundings.

I wanted to block Farshid's voice from entering my ears and my head.

I took a deep breath, reflecting on my father's advice: *positive thoughts create positive energy.*

I wondered what I should say to ignite positive thoughts in Farshid's mind.

'I do not think you are failing,' I said slowly. 'You have been distracted from your studies by so many problems. Do not give up. You need to concentrate on the peer review paper, analyse the results of your surveys, plot the graphs of the data, show it to me then I can comment on it.'

The next morning, I read about the criteria for the ICSE conference papers while Farshid worked on his paper. In the afternoon, he showed me an abstract and some graphs for the new draft versions of both papers. The new one and the one that he showed to his supervisor.

'You read them and tell me which one you like,' Farshid said. 'I will then work on that paper only because time is running out. I can only concentrate on one paper at a time.'

I read them both. As part of Farshid's PhD research project, he had planned to teach online to students from another culture.

'I like the new paper,' I said. 'I think you should include the students in Tam Kỳ and emphasise the cross culture. We can then call it a cross-cultural paper.'

'Ok,' Farshid said. 'That's what I will work on.'

The following day I could see that a good paper was emerging from his work. While Farshid was working on the cross-cultural paper, I searched through the literature and gave him my comments and suggestions.

Two months later when we got home from the hospital after my chemotherapy treatment, Farshid and I received emails from the ICSE that our paper was accepted. Five months later, in May 2019 we travelled to Canada to present two papers at the premier ICSE.

At the Niagara Falls on the way to the ICSE (Software Engineering conference) May 2019.

At the ICSE, Montréal, Canada, May 2019.

While I was treated for breast cancer, to take my mind from negative thoughts, I wrote an academic paper about my experiences in teaching students in Việt Nam. In October 2019, Farshid and I travelled to Việt Nam to meet our students in Tam Kỳ and to take them to the Viet TESOL conference in Huế.

At the Viet TESOL conference, Huế, October 2019.

Taking our online students to the Viet TESOL conference, Huế, October 2019.

Education

The root cause of wrongdoing is ignorance,

and we must therefore hold fast to the tools of perception and knowledge.

Good character must be taught.

Abdu'l-Bahá

Educating the mind without educating the heart is no education at all.

Aristotle

Greek philosopher, 384–322 BC

If a man empties his purse into his head, no man can take it away from him.

An investment in knowledge always pays the best interest.

Ben Franklin, American polymath, 1706–1790

Muốn sang thì bắt cầu kiều,

Muốn cho hay chữ, phải yêu kính thầy.

If you want to cross a river, you must build a bridge,

If you want to learn to read and write, you must love and respect your teacher.

Vietnamese Proverb

Farshid and I planned to have three children together. Despite experiencing five failed attempts at IVF, until the day my period stopped, I had nurtured a hope that one day I would carry our baby inside me.

After three cycles of IVF treatment in Hobart and two cycles in Sydney, Farshid asked, 'Do you want to adopt a child from Việt Nam?'

'No, dear,' I said after some reflection on my mother's life. My mother had adopted two daughters and raised them as her own but both abandoned her when she was sick with MND.

'I love my mother,' I said. 'She left school when she was eight to work to support her family. Her life inspires me to help unfortunate children to get an education so that they can have a better life, but I will never follow her footsteps. I simply cannot devote my time to someone else's child the way she did.'

We decided to provide education to students from disadvantaged backgrounds first through World Vision and later through other ways. We sponsored twelve children in Cambodia, India and Việt Nam through World Vision Australia, donating tens of thousands of dollars over nine years.

In 2007, when we visited two children and the World Vision office in Hà Nội we stopped donating because we saw our donation money was mismanaged. Soon after that we read news that there was wide spread corruption within the World Vision operations over many years in many countries.

Presents for our sponsored students through World Vison (1998–2007).

That year, Farshid and I visited my father's village for the first time. The village head, Thùy, was my cousin. His mother's mother was my father's mother's younger sister.

While travelling through the village with Thùy, I was about to put a large sum of money into a donation box at a temple. Thùy stopped me. 'Your donation should be recognised,' he said. 'They should announce publicly about your donation otherwise it might not reach the people whom you intend to help.'

This had never occurred to me.

I translated what Thùy had said to Farshid and Farshid said, 'that's very good advice.'

I told Thùy about our experiences with our donation to Word Vision.

'If you give those moneys to me,' Thùy said, 'I will announce on the village's loudspeakers and I will give the money to the poor students in presence of the leaders of the school and the village.'

We visited *Trạng Trình*'s Temple in my father's neighbouring village.

'Trạng Trình is his title,' my father said. 'His name is Nguyễn Bỉnh Khiêm. He was the king's highest scholarly adviser, but he left his position and came back here. He built the Bạch Vân Am and Quán Trung Tân and divided his estate into eighteen Am, teaching literature. After him many scholars continued to encourage others to maintain the spirit of learning. His ancestral village is Trung Am. During his time, Trung Am, our village Tiên Am and the sixteen other Am were under his care.'

We went to a teashop. We sat at a low table with matching small chairs. The shopkeeper invited my father to smoke *thuốc lào* in the Vietnamese traditional tobacco pipe. My father thanked the shopkeeper then turned to me and said, 'This place reminds me of your grandparents. They could afford to send me to Vinh for primary and high school education by selling thuốc lào. Your grandfather always brought his own thuốc lào leaves with him. He carried them in his belt, *ruột tượng* (literally meaning an elephant's intestine) which he wore underneath his áo dài. It was a long piece of cloth wrapped around his waist in which he kept money and essential items.'

'Our village and seventeen other villages had special names,' my father said. 'In the whole of Việt Nam, until now only Nguyễn Bỉnh Khiêm divided his property into eighteen different *Am* and named them as such. The word Am means pagoda or small temple. Each name conveys a special meaning: *Trung Am* means the Loyalty Pagoda; *Tiên Am*, the Forebear Pagoda; *Cổ Am*, the Ancient Pagoda; *Bào Am*, the Brotherhood Pagoda. People in this region respect him greatly. When I was a child, your grandfather told me that Trạng Trình Nguyễn Bỉnh Khiêm was the greatest scholar and the foremost teacher.'

After visiting Trạng Trình's Temple, I told Thùy that Farshid and I would like to give to the poor elders and poor students some money and Australian T-shirts which we had brought from Sydney as our gesture wishing them happy *Tết* of the Year of the Pig.

Thùy immediately gathered the leaders of the village and the principals of the village schools to welcome us. They gave us flowers and a lacquer painting with mother of pearl inlay of Trạng Trình Nguyễn Bỉnh Khiêm. Farshid and I greatly appreciated their warm welcome and we were touched by the actions of the village community.

Receiving flowers and a painting with mother of pearl inlay of Trạng Trình Nguyễn Bỉnh Khiêm from the Leader of the Communist Party and Village Head Thùy, Tiên Am (Xã Vĩnh Tiến), Vĩnh Bảo, 2007.

Minh Hiền standing with her father, the Leader of the Communist Party, the Principal of the village high school, Thùy, students, village elders; Farshid sitting with Minh Hiền's uncle and the village eldest lady at her ancestral village Tiên Am, 2007.

With high school students, the principal of the high school, the deputy village head, the village head Thùy and the leader of the communist party at their school in the village, 2007.

With students at the Village Hall, 2007.

When we returned to Australia we directly sent money to Việt Nam to support poor children in schools and to the University of Tasmania to support refugee students.

We provided scholarships to refugee students at the University of Tasmania from 2008 to 2014.

Meeting refugee students at the University of Tasmania for lunch, 2009.

We visited the village in Việt Nam and the University of Tasmania regularly to give scholarships to the students.

For nine years from Tết 2007 to 2016, we sponsored students from kindergarten to grade nine for their education and gave awards to students who earned top marks in either mathematics or literature in each grade.

When we could not go to Việt Nam, I sent money to Thùy to organise the award ceremonies with the teachers and principals of three schools: a kindergarten, a primary and a junior high school.

Thùy took a lot of photos and sent them to us. I would collect his registered letters from our post office on the way to work. In the group photos, there are rows of students from the three schools, standing in front of an award banner with our names as sponsors of the awards, the year and the school term of the ceremony. They stand with the principal of their school, the deputy village head, the village head Thùy and the leader of the communist party.

The students wear *khăn quàng đỏ* red scarf around their neck, each holding a large envelop and smiling as if they were standing in front of me, gazing at me. Seeing their happy faces warms my heart.

LỄ PHÁT THƯỞNG CHO CÁC CHÁU NGHÈO TRƯỜNG MẦM NON XÃ VĨNH TIẾN . 2007 - 2008

LÃNH ĐẠO ĐỊA PHƯƠNG . CÙNG CÁC BAN NGHÀNH . CÁC THẦY CÔ GIÁO CỦA 3 TRƯỜNG - NHÂN NGÀY PHÁT THƯỞNG HỌC BỔNG CỦA NHÀ TÀI TRỢ - MINH HIỀN - FA RSHID

When we visited the village high school in 2009, we saw that they had only an old computer so we bought them a new computer. The whole school and Thùy appreciated our humble gift.

With high school principal, Thùy and teachers and students at the village school, 2009.

With primary and high school students at the village school, 2009.

With primary school students at the village school, 2009.

Village leaders, principals and students, 2009.

Village leaders, principals and students, 2009.

Village leaders, principals and students, 2010.

Village leaders, principals and students, 2010.

HỌC SINH GIỎI VÀ NGHÈO VƯỢT KHÓ
TRƯỜNG TIỂU HỌC KỲ I 2009-2010

HỌC SINH GIỎI T T HỌC CƠ SỞ
KỲI 2009-2010

HỌC SINH NGHÈO VƯỢT KHÓ
TRƯỜNG TRUNG HỌC CƠ SỞ KỲ I 2009-2010

HỌC SINH GIỎI MÔN TOÁN VĂN
TRƯỜNG TRUNG HỌC CƠ SỞ KỲ I 2009-2010

Village leaders, principals and students, 2010.

In 2013, we visited the village after the 4th International Conference on Information Systems Management and Evaluation (ICIME) in Sài Gòn.

With primary and high school students at the Village Primary School, 2013.

In 2014, we visited the village after travelling to Ghent, Belgium, for the 2014 European Conference on IS Management and Evaluation (ECIME).

At Tiên Am (now Xã Vĩnh Tiến), Vĩnh Bảo, 2014.

At Tiên Am (now Xã Vĩnh Tiến), Vĩnh Bảo, 2014.

At Tiên Am (now Xã Vĩnh Tiến), Vĩnh Bảo, 2014.

In 2016, we visited the village after the 8th International Conference on Computer Research and Development, ICCRD, in Nha Trang.

At Tiên Am (now Xã Vĩnh Tiến), Vĩnh Bảo, 2016.

At Tiên Am (now Xã Vĩnh Tiến), Vĩnh Bảo, 2016.

In 2016, Thùy retired. The leaders of the village and the principals of the village schools were also changed. The new high school principal did not wish us to meet his students. He expected us to send our money to him and it was up to him and other leaders to decide how to allocate the money and for whom. Farshid and I stopped providing the scholarships to the village students.

Supporting students of Baha'i families

After giving our last scholarships to the village students we visited the local Baha'i communities in Phan Thiết and Đà Nẵng and provided scholarships to students there.

Phan Thiết, 2016.

Đà Nẵng, 2016.

Đà Nẵng, 2016.

Đà Nẵng, 2017.

Cộng đồng Tôn giáo Baha'i Đà Nẵng
THÁNH LỄ GIÁNG SINH SONG HÀNH CỦA ĐỨC BAHA'U'LL
KỶ NIỆM 200 NĂM GIÁNG SINH ĐỨC BAH
(1817-2017)

Wealthy Me Academy

Regard man as a mine rich in gems of inestimable value. Education can, alone, cause it to reveal its treasures, and enable mankind to benefit therefrom.

Bahá'u'lláh

An investment in knowledge pays the best interest.

Benjamin Franklin, American polymath, 1706- 1790

Learning is not attained by chance,

it must be sought for with ardor and diligence.

Abigail Adams, the second first lady of the United States, 1744–1818

On 3 December 2018, the United Nations General Assembly proclaimed 24 January as International Day of Education in celebration of the role of education for peace and development. Education is considered the fundamental right of a person. This day is dedicated towards promoting the role of education in our lives.

The theme for International Day of Education in 2019 was *Education: A Key Driver for Inclusion and Empowerment*. In 2020 the theme was *Learning for People, Planet, Prosperity, and Peace*. In 2021 the theme was *Recover and Revitalize Education for the COVID-19 Generation*. In 2022 the theme was *Changing Course, Transforming Education*. In 2023 the theme was *Investing in People, Prioritizing Education*. In 2024 the theme was *Learning for Lasting Peace*.

In 2016, reflecting on our experiences of providing scholarships and money to poor students through various organisations and after our experiences with the village, we decided that the best option to help students in rural areas of Việt Nam was to teach them English, IT and accounting enabling them to earn a decent salary for themselves.

By that time I had taught thousands of students and university staff over many years. Farshid and I had presented many academic papers in learning and teaching at international conferences.

We decided to name our teaching activities *Wealthy Me Academy*. We decided that through *Wealthy Me Academy* we would encourage young people to achieve wealth through education. We would teach students from disadvantaged background what we know. We would share our experiences to promote wealthy thoughts and encourage learning.

In November 2017, when we presented our paper at the Quảng Nam University in Tam Kỳ, we decided to teach IT and accounting to students at the university because most students were from rural or minority background. Their knowledge of English and finance was very limited so we decided to teach English, the reflective concept and basic finance to students. We met Mrs Phan Thị Diệu Hiền at Quảng Nam University, She requested us to teach her students. In 2018 we taught second year students online via Facebook (Class 2017-2018). Class 2017-2018 consisted of students who were in the second semester of their second year of their university course. This was the first online course which we delivered from Australia to Vietnamese students. Our aim was to provide students, in remote areas of Việt Nam, an opportunity to communicate with and to learn English from us and other educators who are living in Western countries such as Australia.

We offered every student in Mrs Diệu Hiền's second-year English class a chance to participate in a five-week online study. Forty students took part in the studies. Thirty-five students completed all the study requirements. We presented papers about our teaching experience at the 5th International Conference on *Language, Society and Culture in Asian Contexts* (LSCAC) in Huế in May 2018.

At the Language, Society and Culture in Asian Contexts (LSCAC) conference, Huế, 2018.

Since then we have delivered online courses to students at Quảng Nam University every year and we presented papers about our teaching experience at the 5th Viet TESOL International Convention in Huế in October 2019, the 7th Viet TESOL International Convention, virtual, hosted by Vinh University, in October 2021, the 8th Viet TESOL International Convention, virtual, hosted by Nha Trang University, in September 2022, the 9th Viet TESOL International Convention, hosted by the People's Security Academy in Hà Nội in August 2023, and the 12th Open TESOL International Conference, hosted by the Hồ Chí Minh City Open University in Sài Gòn in May 2024.

In all our courses we use videos from various sources such as *Oxford Online English*, *Grammar Videos* from the *British Council*, *Every day English* from the *ABC TV Education in Australia*. Since January 2024, we have included videos of Ms Margaret Eldridge reading from the texts that we prepared. Our students found Margaret's videos very useful. In October 2024, Ngọc Hiền, our second-year student, posted: "Mrs. Margaret Eldridge reads slowly and clearly so I can understand the content of the video." In January 2024, Vân Ly, our first-year student, posted: "Margaret Eldridge reads very fluently. I can detect stress in a word. Because I had read the article about Minh, I was able to detect the vocabulary. I can hear voices rising and falling. I had to listen to it many times and I found the British English accent very good. I tried saying the same but it was difficult. After listening I want to learn British English it makes me very excited."

In May 2018, when we presented a paper at the LSCAC conference in Huế, we celebrated my 55th birthday with Diệu Hiền, Tố Nga and Vinh Linh from Quảng Nam University. Farshid and I enjoyed these occasions. We had no ideas that I had breast cancer at the time.

My 55th birthday celebration, Huế, 2018.

After successfully teaching students of class of 2017-2018 online using Facebook, we developed our course further using the online learning and teaching application, called Moodle.

We taught a new cohort of second-year students during 2018-2019. We taught two courses of nine-week duration each. The students learnt with us while I was treated with breast cancer. They knew nothing about my treatment as I did not want them to be worried.

In September 2019 we came to Tam Kỳ to meet the students. We awarded all students who completed our course with certificates.

In October 2019 we presented a paper and a workshop of our teaching experiences at the Viet TESOL International Convention in Huế. We sponsored ten students who completed our two nine-week courses with a trip to Huế to attend the convention and to celebrate their success with us.

With our online students, Tam Kỳ, 2019.

With our online students, Huế, 2019.

In 2020, the principal of the Quảng Nam University invited us to present our paper at the research discussion seminar. Due to the Covid-19 pandemic we sent the university our paper and it was published by the university.

Throughout the Covid-19 pandemic we continued teaching Quảng Nam University students online.

In 2021 and 2022, we delivered oral presentations at the Virtual Viet TESOL International Conventions hosted by Vinh University and Nha Trang University, respectively.

Because of the Covid-19 lockdown, we could not meet any students until September 2023 when we travelled to the Viet TESOL International Conventions in Việt Nam.

We presented two papers at the 9th Viet TESOL International Convention, hosted in Hà Nội from August 25 to August 27, 2023 by the Ministry of Public Security's People's Security Academy in collaboration with the Ministry of Education and Training (MOET)'s National Foreign Language Project and Viet TESOL Association.

At the Viet TESOL International Convention, Hà Nội, August 2023.

In 2024, we met our online students in Tam Kỳ and in Đà Nẵng.

We presented a paper about our teaching experience and the progress of our students, titled *Promoting Learner Autonomy and Intercultural Competence Through Reflective Learning among First-year Students: an Action Research*, at the 12th Open TESOL International Conference held at Hồ Chí Minh City Open University on 24–25 May 2024.

At the Open TESOL Conference, Sài Gòn, May 2024.

Teaching

Teaching is the highest form of understanding.

Aristotle, Greek philosopher and polymath, 384-322 BC.

Give a man a fish and you feed him for a day;

teach a man to fish and you feed him for a lifetime.

Maimonides, Spanish Philosopher, 1135-1204.

At the *International Conference on Computer Research and Development* to present a paper about our designing teaching applications, Nha Trang, Việt Nam, 2016.

In 2016, we went to Nha Trang to present an IT paper about our designing of online teaching applications, titled *A Five-Dimensional Requirements Elicitation Framework for e-Learning Systems*. By that time, we had presented many academic papers at international conferences about learning and teaching. However, it was this trip that made us realise that the best way for us to help Vietnamese students from remote areas is to teach them ourselves.

Teaching our students in the library of the Quảng Nam University, September 2019.

Teaching our students in the hotel, Tam Kỳ, September 2019.

Achievements of Class 2018-2019

Reflecting on our experience of teaching during 2018-2019, we extended our courses to nine weeks. Class 2018-2019 consisted of students who started to study with us in 2018 when they were in the first semester of their second year of their university course. Forty students enrolled in our first-level course, thirty-five students completed. Twelve students continued to the next level course and ten completed the level-two course during the second semester of their second-year university.

At the end of the second course with us, two students, Lê Hoàng Yến and Lê Yến Nhi, wrote an article which was published in May 2019 by Quảng Nam University as part of the university's research activities. They wrote: "We can confidently use our English language skills in the classroom as well as outside the classroom. Now each time we do our homework, we make less grammatical mistakes and use English words correctly matching the situation. The course not only has helped us gain knowledge, but also we have more practical experience, such as how to create a short but effective interview and how to work well in groups, We know that people have different personalities and are different in the ways they work in different environments. We also learned how to make, manage and use money appropriately."

In 2019, we celebrated with the students in Tam Kỳ. The photo shows the ten students who completed our two courses and travelled with us to Huế for the Viet TESOL international convention.

Celebrations with our online students, Tam Kỳ, September 2019.

With our online students at the Viet TESOL convention in October 2019 in Huế.

Celebratory dinner with our online students, Huế, 2019.

Students attending *Chùa Thiên Mụ*, Huế, 2019.

On the *Hương River* on the way to *Chùa Thiên Mụ*, Huế, 2019.

On the *Tràng Tiền Bridge*, Huế, 2019.

Minh Hiền with Nguyễn Diệp Trinh on the Hương River to Chuà Thiên Mụ (2019).

Diệp Trinh thanked us for providing her with an opportunity to attend the 2019 Viet TESOL International Convention in Huế. She said that she learnt a lot from our online courses and she found the Viet TESOL convention and the trip to Huế very meaningful.

Diệp Trinh graduated with honours in English from the Quảng Nam University in July 2021. She was born and raised in Quảng Nam. She said that her hometown has many interesting things and many beautiful scenes, however what she likes the most about her hometown is the people; they are very enthusiastic and fun loving.

During 2021 and 2022 because of the Covid-19 Pandemic, there were limited job opportunities. However when she was in her final year at Quảng Nam University, she worked as an intern at the PopoDoo English Center which gave her some teaching expereince. She set up classes at her home to teach English to children from four to ten years old. The children loved her and were eager to learn. Their appreciations made her very happy.

She thinks that teaching is a good profession and she wants to become a good English teacher.

She is now married and lives in Đà Nẵng.

In 2024, we met her, her husband and one-year-old daughter.

She is now teaching at the pre-school which her daughter attends.

With Diệp Trinh and her family, Đà Nẵng, 2024.

Achievements of Classes 2020-2021 and 2021-2022

Our teaching activities consist of four courses at four levels. Students' participations are outside their university classes and they are free to participate or not. Students who complete the previous level course are allowed to study the next level course.

Class 2020-2021 consists of students who started studying with us in April 2021 when they were in the second semester of their first year of their university. Thirteen first-year students participated. Six students completed the level-one course in June 2021. Of these six students, five students completed the level-two course in June 2022.

Class 2021-2022 consists of students who started studying with us in March 2022 when they were first-year students. Twelve first-year students participated. Five completed the level-one course in June 2022.

While teaching we observed that many students worked hard and some students had to work after hours while studying so that they could afford to pay their university fees.

In 2022, we decided to give scholarships to those who completed our courses. In November 2022, ten students received our scholarships: five first-year students from class 2021-2022 and five second-year students from class 2020-2021. Due to the Covid-19 lockdown we could not go to Việt Nam. We sent money to the university to give to the students on our behalf.

Students of Classes 2020-2021 and 2021-2022, Tam Kỳ, 2022. Photo courtesy of Diệu Hiền.

Class 2020-2021

After the Covid-19 lockdown, in 2023 we travelled to Tam Kỳ to meet our online students and to give scholarships to those who completed our courses.

With Class 2020-2021 students, Tam Kỳ, 2023.

With Class 2020-2021 students, Tam Kỳ, 2024.

Hồ Thị Thu Trúc started studying with us in April 2021. She studied online with us throughout the Covid-19 pandemic. Thu Trúc posted at the end of her third course: "First and foremost, I would like to say thank you to the teachers for giving me the opportunity to join this course. I have had chances to approach a new format and a scientific method of learning English. After this course, my English has improved a lot, I have more awareness of grammar thanks to many useful grammatical videos, and I feel more confident when I speak." She completed our fourth course in April 2024. While studying at university, she worked between thirty and fifty hours a week teaching English to primary and high school students. She graduated in June 2024. She is a confident and determined young lady. We are very pleased with her progress.

Class 2021-2022

With Class 2021-2022 students, Tam Kỳ, 2023.

With Anh Thư of Class 2022-2023 and students of Class 2021-2022
Tam Thanh Beach, Tam Kỳ, 2023.

From left to right Tâm, Anh Thư, Minh Hiền and Thảo Linh, Tam Kỳ, 2024.

Class 2021-2022 Trần Vương Hải Anh, Lê Thị Thảo Linh and Hồ Thị Tâm started studying with us in March 2022. They were very keen to study with us. They spent their summer break studying our level-four course and completed it in August 2024. We are pleased with their progress.

At the end of the third course:

Hải Anh posted, "The online learning journey with teachers and courses on the web is an emotionally rich experience. The ability to connect with instructors and immerse myself in course content through the online environment not only brings convenience but also fosters an atmosphere of emotional warmth and closeness. This flexibility not only opens doors to learning from anywhere but also helps me build a special connection with the learning process, where emotions and knowledge converge, creating a memorable learning journey. I look forward to the possibility of continuing this educational adventure with dedicated and inspiring teachers in the future."

Thảo Linh posted: "Learning is learning more, learning forever, that is very important in our lives. And now, I have a very useful and interesting course. I have been practicing and studying hard every day. That is to improve listening, speaking, reading, writing skills and practice confidence when standing in front of the camera. I am grateful for the enthusiastic attention and online website. I sincerely thank the teachers for creating this course, to connect friends and teachers to become closer. I hope that the course will last forever, from generation to generation, so that everyone can learn."

Tâm posted: "I would like to express my genuine enthusiasm at the prospect of continuing my studies with you in the future, especially through an online course. Every lesson with you is an experience filled with novelty and I find myself eagerly looking forward to each new topic we will learn about.

The excitement I felt didn't just come from the joy of learning. It was a tangible growth that I witnessed in myself, a growth that was recognized by both my peers and especially my teachers. My progress has boosted my confidence significantly. This affirmation has become a strong motivation, motivating me to accept challenges with the spirit of learning and making further progress.

When I was about to graduate, taking an online course under your guidance made a deep impression on me. I believe that this additional opportunity will not only enhance my knowledge but also help me be more prepared for the challenges ahead after graduation. Your teaching style and mentorship are invaluable and I look forward to continuing this journey of academic and personal development under your guidance.

Thank you for being an inspiration and I look forward to continue studying with you in the future."

Hải Anh and Thảo Linh plan to become English teachers. They have started teaching primary students at home during their summer break.

Tâm plans to work as a tour guide while teaching young students after hours.

We wish them success.

Achievements of Class 2022-2023

Class 2022-2023 consists of students who started studying with us in March 2023 when they were in the second semester of their first year of their university course. Fourteen students participated. Four students completed our level-one course. In 2023, we met our students at the highest room in the highest hotel in Tam Kỳ. We chose that place because we knew that our students had never been there and we wanted them to experience the beauty of their city.

With teachers Diệu Hiền, Vinh Linh and Quảng Nam University students of Classes 2020-2021, 2021-2022 and 2022-2023, Tam Kỳ, 2023.

Class 2022-2023 from left to right: Ngọc Trâm, Tuyết Sương, Minh Hiền, Anh Thư, Thùy Trang, 2023.

With Quảng Nam University students of Class 2022-2023, Tam Kỳ, 2023.

With Anh Thư, Thùy Trang and Tuyết Sương of Class 2022-2023, Tam Kỳ, 2024.

Hùynh Anh Thư, Nguyễn Thị Tuyết Sương and Xa Thị Thùy Trang completed the level-two course in June 2024.

They were very keen when studying with us. They spent their summer break studying our level-three course and completed it in August 2024.

After meeting us, Anh Thư posted her writing for the topic *to describe a hotel that you know*, as follows: "Although I haven't experienced the rooms personally, I can speak highly of the top floor, which is the 20th floor. This is a special area designed for meetings and gatherings. I had the pleasure of experiencing this space with my friends through an online course. The view from the top floor is breath taking, offering a panoramic vista of the vast and beautiful city of Tam Ky. It was an unforgettable experience to stand there, taking in the expansive cityscape.

What makes this hotel particularly special to me is that it was the place where I met my teachers, Farshid and Minh Hien, Ms Dieu Hien, along with friends from my online course. We spent quality time together, engaging in enriching conversations, and sharing valuable knowledge. These interactions were incredibly beneficial, and the memories made at Muong Thanh Hotel are ones I cherish deeply."

At the end of the level-three course,

Anh Thư posted: "I feel extremely grateful for having the opportunity to participate in this course. The course has brought me so many benefits, such as learning new vocabulary, reviewing grammar structures, improving my listening and speaking skills, and gaining new knowledge that I had never known before. Additionally, the course has helped me develop a habit of daily practice and the detailed feedback from the teacher has been incredibly helpful in my learning process. I believe that the interactive and supportive learning environment this course provides will greatly enhance my learning experience. Thank you for offering such a valuable course, and I look forward to the opportunity to study with you in the future."

Thùy Trang posted: "I am very interested in taking your online course because I believe it will bring a lot of value to choose my personal and professional development. In particular, I look forward to learning more about new skills, knowledge. I realize that continuous learning is essential to development. I look forward to having a flexible learning environment, suitable for my busy work schedule. I also appreciate the high quality learning and learning materials that you provide, helping me to continue to build formulas effectively and apply them in practice. I hope the next course will give me more experiences to continue to improve myself to be more perfect. Thank you very much, teachers."

Tuyết Sương posted: "For me personally, I want to study and accompany you. A very good online learning app, full of experience and knowledge. Supplementing additional knowledge is convenient for my school studies. In addition, the online course also trains me in many virtues. I like to study this course, studying every working day and studying every day will be very good. Instead of giving up, I try harder. But there is one thing I am afraid of, in the near future I will be a Junior, and will start an internship. I am afraid that I will not have regular time to do the course work. But I will still try to arrange to study and accompany Dr. Farshid and Ms. Minh Hien. For me, this course is very meaningful, it has changed me in the most remarkable way. From a lazy student, not studious. Becoming a more diligent person, more eager to learn and love English more. I have a great experience, so I really want to learn more."

We are pleased with their progress. We will teach them our level-four course in 2025.

Achievements of Class 2023-2024

Class 2023-2024 consists of students who started studying with us in January 2024 when they were in the second semester of their first year of their university course.

In 2024, eighteen first-year students from Quảng Nam University and Đà Nẵng University participated. Four students completed the level-one course: two from Quảng Nam University and two from Đà Nẵng University.

With teachers Diệu Hiền, Vinh Linh and Quảng Nam University students of Classes 2020-2021, 2021-2022, 2022-2023 and 2023-2024, Tam Kỳ, 2024.

At the end of the level-one course, A Viết Vân Ly from Quảng Nam University posted: "I am very happy to participate in this course. I found it very useful. When the teachers in the course gave feedback, I gained a little more knowledge. Through this course, I learned about the five-dimensional reflective cycle framework. If there is an opportunity to study for free like this, why would not I take it? If there are no problems, I will continue to take the course. I realized that studying the course helped me be much more diligent and persistent."

Blúp Lưu from Quảng Nam University posted: "If I have the opportunity, I will continue to study this course, because the teachers are very enthusiastic and thoughtful with students, teach very thoughtfully and have many really useful things. Taking an online course like this is quite difficult to work hard at, but after completing it, the students have trained themselves to persevere and know "nothing is impossible". Just believe in yourself and you can do it all. Thank you for letting me participate in this course. Thanks a lot."

With Quảng Nam University students of Class 2023-2024, Tam Kỳ, 2024.

With Vân Ly and Blúp Lưu of Class 2023-2024, Tam Kỳ, 2024.

With Vân Ly, Tam Kỳ, 2024. Photo courtesy of Blúp Lưu.

In 2023, we met teacher Ngàn Thương and she introduced her students to our course. They were first-year students of Primary Education at Đà Nẵng University.

Since January 2024, we also taught students from Đà Nẵng University.

With teacher Ngàn Thương and Đà Nẵng University students of Class 2023-2024
Đà Nẵng, 2024.

Minh Hiền with Bùi Thị Tuyết Mai and Phan Thị Ngọc Hiền of Đà Nẵng University Class 2023-2024, Đà Nẵng, 2024.

At the end of the level-one course, Ngọc Hiền posted: "If I have the opportunity, I want to continue to study this English course. Because I know many friends from this course. Moreover, teachers are very enthusiastic and kind, they provide me a lot of useful knowledge. They show me more love for English. That makes me more interested in learning English. So I want to learn more from teachers to know more things about English. Thank you for giving me a useful English course."

Vân Ly, Blúp Lưu and Ngọc Hiền have continued to study with us. They completed the level-two course in November 2024.

Peace Education Freedom

At the age of seventeen, I left my motherland for Australia in a fishing boat. I took the greatest risk of my life, to step into that tiny wooden fishing boat for *peace*, *education* and *freedom*.

Peace, I have. Australia is a peaceful country. No war here.

Education, I have.

> One day my eldest brother Tri noticing a new certificate on the wall in my home, he asked, 'Are you collecting stamps?'
>
> I smiled at his remark. It was within my nature that whatever I did, I gave it my best effort.
>
> When I could not get a job as an engineer after I graduated with Honours, I studied for a Master of Engineering Science.
>
> When I worked for an insurance company writing computing programs to solve money matters, I took the initiative to study accounting to better understand the needs of the company and its customers.
>
> When I was made redundant from a job at the Hydro, I studied for a Master of Commerce before leaving Hobart.
>
> When I worked for a banking company in Sydney, I enrolled for a management course to learn how to manage projects better.
>
> When I was made redundant after I was assaulted by a drunken man, I enrolled for a Master of Arts in Creative Writing in order to write books.
>
> While working at a university in Sydney, I completed three subjects of a Diploma in Law and a Master of Higher Education. I had chosen to complete a Master of Higher Education over a Diploma in Law because I wanted to gain an understanding of higher education and to teach better. During my personal time I conducted research on how adults learn. The topics of my research were the effects of personality on learning and how best to design course materials to teach people with different personality traits and knowledge. I studied in the evenings. I studied on the bus while travelling to work. I conducted research and wrote papers during weekends. I took annual leave to present papers at international conferences held in Australia, Europe and Asia.
>
> While teaching English to students at the Quảng Nam University, I studied for a Master of Education. I wanted to make sure that I had good knowledge of educational studies to teach my students. Through the studies, I had a better understanding of how students learn and their needs and, I developed learning materials for my students accordingly.

Freedom, I have and I believe that we can only have freedom when we have peace and education.

The day I left my childhood home, my father said, 'Don't abandon your studies. No one can take away your understanding and your knowledge, but cruel people can take away your money and position.' My father was right.

I feel fortunate that I have peace, education and freedom.

Thảnh thơi dưới ánh chiều tà

Ung dung đọc sách nhớ ngày tháng qua

Ao kia cũng có cội nguồn

Đời người ai chẳng khi buồn lúc vui

Đây là một mảnh đời tôi

Tương lai trước mặt cội nguồn mãi thương.

Trí Tuệ Trần (Minh Hiền's elder brother)

Relaxing under the western sun,

Leisurely reading 'My Heritage',

Nostalgic about the good old days,

Even the lake has its heritage,

Life is joy and of course sorrow,

Here's a piece of my life,

A bright future always springs up from the lovely roots.

Translated by Minh Hiền

Minh Hiền exactly one year after her last chemotherapy session, January 2020.

Acknowledgements

We thank Margaret Eldridge AM for proofreading this book and writing the foreword.

We thank Minh Hiền's niece, Ellyse Tran, for the paintings that she created especially for Minh Hiền.

We thank Minh Hiền's elder brother, Trí Tuệ Trần, for composing the poem.

We thank our students for participating in our courses and for giving consent for us to use their data and to quote them.

We thank Bảo, the youngest son of Minh Hiền's father's friend Mr Xiêm for taking Minh Hiền photo in the Singapore Refugee Camp in 1981.

We thank Dr Xuân (Susan) Đào, Mrs Phan Thị Diệu Hiền and our student Blúp Lưu for taking the photos as noted in the captions of the photos.

Every effort has been made to trace copyright holders of the photographic material included in this book. We would appreciate hearing from any copyright holders not here acknowledged.

Minh Hiền with her online students, Tam Kỳ, 19 September 2019

www.ingramcontent.com/pod-product-compliance
Lightning Source LLC
Chambersburg PA
CBHW040300100426
42811CB00011B/1325

* 9 7 8 0 6 4 5 9 7 8 2 2 3 *